Transforming Your Outdoor Early Learning Environment

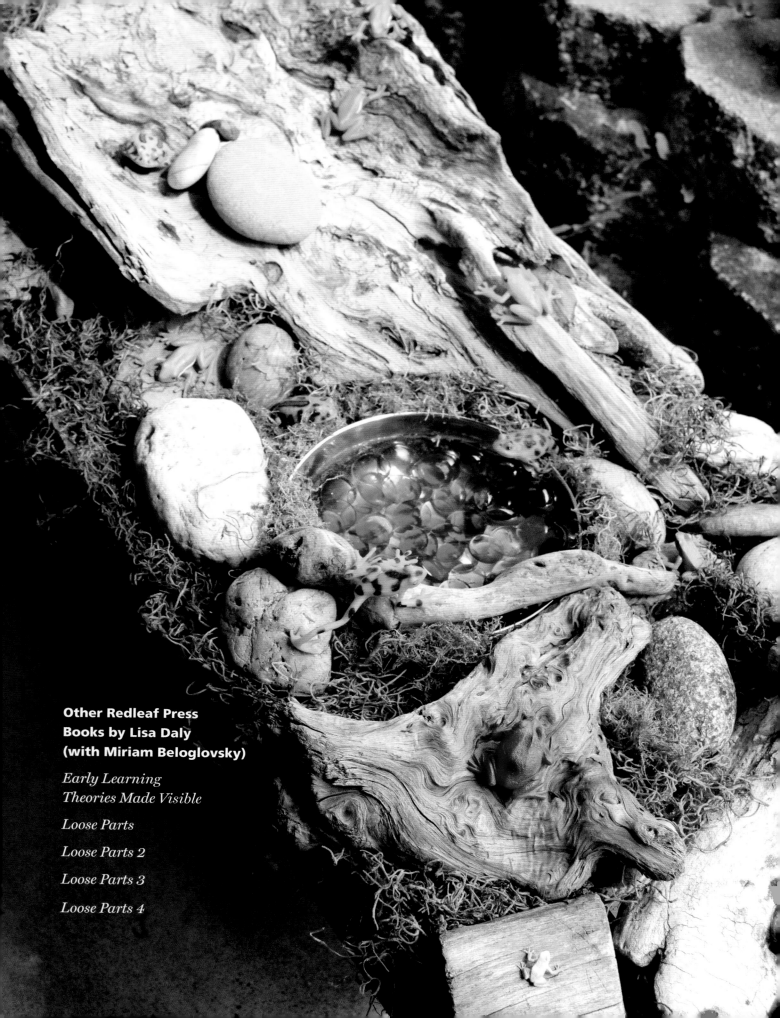

**Other Redleaf Press
Books by Lisa Daly
(with Miriam Beloglovsky)**

*Early Learning
Theories Made Visible*

Loose Parts

Loose Parts 2

Loose Parts 3

Loose Parts 4

Transforming Your Outdoor Early Learning Environment

LISA DALY

Redleaf Press®
www.redleafpress.org
800-423-8309

Published by Redleaf Press
10 Yorkton Court
St. Paul, MN 55117
www.redleafpress.org

First edition 2022
Cover design by Renee Hammes
Cover photographs by Jenna Knight
Interior design by Erin Kirk
Typeset in Miller Text Roman
Interior photos by Jenna Knight
Printed in the United States of America
28   27   26   25   24   23   22   21   1   2   3   4   5   6   7   8

Library of Congress Cataloging-in-Publication Data

Names: Daly, Lisa, author.
Title: Transforming your outdoor early learning environment / by Lisa Daly.
Description: First edition. | St. Paul, MN : Redleaf Press, 2021. | Includes bibliographical references. | Summary: "Transforming Your Outdoor Early Learning Environments invites center and home-based educators to reimagine and reconstruct their image of conventional children's play yards as they know them and to create beautiful outdoor learning spaces on a limited budget with natural elements and loose parts that offer children opportunity for irresistible engaging explorations. Ideas, inspiration, and benefits for changing outdoor environments are provided along with the basics for designing, transforming, and maintaining 11 specific outdoor play zones"— Provided by publisher.
Identifiers: LCCN 2021034954 (print) | LCCN 2021034955 (ebook) | ISBN 9781605547381 (paperback) | ISBN 9781605547398 (ebook)
Subjects: LCSH: Play environments. | Early childhood education—Activity programs.
Classification: LCC LB1139.35.P55 D374 2021 (print) | LCC LB1139.35.P55 (ebook) | DDC 372.21--dc23
LC record available at https://lccn.loc.gov/2021034954
LC ebook record available at https://lccn.loc.gov/2021034955

Printed on acid-free paper

For my parents, Don and Lois,
who give me love, time, encouragement,
validation, hope, guidance, and
wisdom unconditionally.

Contents

Acknowledgments

I want to thank the many educators who welcomed me into your programs, generously engaged in incredible work to transform your thinking, and significantly supported efforts to transform outdoor environments into captivating play spaces for children. I am grateful for the many friendships and meaningful relationships that I have made along the way.

I want to offer special thanks to the individuals who allowed photography in their wonderful programs: Melissa Baker, Heather Butler, and Donna Elmore at Valley Oak Children's Services; Ivory Gross at Little Kids on the Block; Meuy Wang Family Child Care; Kellie Farrell, Kerry Venegas, Lesli Nieto, and Jeanine Canedo-Moncrief at Changing Tide Family Services; Nina Surbaugh at Acorns to Oaks Child Care; Ana Tejeda Child Care Home; Karen Thomas at Karen's Family Child Care; Morgan Kelley at Little Willow Preschool; Wendy Walter at Wendy's Family Child Care; Lori and Jim Bistodeau at Florence; Lisa Taub at The Early Years School; Shawn Edwinson at Bright Beginnings Preschool; and Rosie and Paul Licata at Little Shapes Bilingual Preschool.

I am especially grateful to several agencies that afforded me the opportunity to collaborate with program educators in a reflective process to transform their environments. I am thankful to the educators and administrators for their trust, willingness to risk, and support of my effort to transform and photograph environments. In each case, the result was a thoughtfully designed outdoor environment that includes amazing, fascinating, and beautiful spaces for children, families, and educators. These individuals include Clara Nakai, coordinator of EHS/FCCH at Modesto City Schools; Maggie and Randy Smith at Next Steps Family Day Care; Yolande Nichols; Louis Vargas at Babalous Daycare; Armida Kaun, Jennifer Vasquez, Kimberly Lister, Lindsay Prestwich, and Nicole Hall at the California Department of Education, Early Learning and Care Division;

Gloreta Johnson and educators at Park West and Wishon Hansel & Gretel Day Cares; Sarah Van Lieu at Small Wonders Childcare; and Kimberly Butcher at Honcut Early Head Start.

To all the parents, thank you for allowing your children's engagement in meaningful experiences to be captured in photographs and shared as an educational resource. Getting to know your children and observing their investigations and relationships was a delight and pleasure.

Nina, Maggie, Lisa, Rosie, and Paul, your programs abound with creativity, beauty, and innovation. It warms my heart to receive inspiring photos of children's engagement with new design ideas in your marvelous environments.

Nicole Braun and Aubrey Greene at Creative Spirit Learning Center, you truly are ambassadors of play. Your program is magical and a place of wonder, discovery, joy, and belonging. Thank you for your ingenuity and the work that you do to make a difference in the lives of children and families.

Cheri Quishenbery, I cannot begin to thank you for partnering with me on so many amazing adventures. Your energy, creativity, inspiration, and passion are infectious. Everyone who visits your program marvels at surprising features hidden around every corner and how capable and competent the children are. You have created an environment that is truly special. I treasure our friendship and appreciate you more than you will ever know. I look forward to new journeys with you.

Jenna, thank you for being my reflective partner. I value your perspective and innovative spirit. My heartfelt thanks to you for sharing your photography talent, thinking, time, and expertise. This project would not have been possible without you.

Dan, there are no words to express how blessed I am for your continued support and encouragement. Thank you for always being there. I am so grateful you are in my life.

Introduction to *Transforming Your Outdoor Early Learning Environment*

Visiting early childhood practicum students in a wide variety of environments has been one of my pleasures and passions. One program is quaint and welcoming, while another is filled with rich play opportunities for children. I never know until I arrive what the program's characteristics will be. I find that I am drawn to imperfect programs, but the feel and environment are important. A good program, I have determined over the years, must always be filled with joy, warmth, connections, a sense of belonging, flexible spaces, intriguing loose parts, engagement, risk, reflection, and intentional educators. That is quite a list of qualities, and they are not seen in every program.

Unfortunately, today is one of those days when I am observing a program that lacks many of these qualities. Upon my arrival, I am escorted to an outdoor play space that is hot and narrow with an asphalt surface. A few random plastic toys clutter the area. The air is filled with arguing as 12 children compete for limited plastic riding toys. Lucky children attempt to maneuver riding toys in the limited space. Some children run around aimlessly while two children stand and stare. There is no evidence of the natural world. The practicum student tries to remain positive, but she assumes an authoritarian role as she strives to maintain some sense of order. My heart aches for the children, families, and teachers of this program. It does not have to be this way. Simple ways exist to transform sterile outdoor areas into beautiful, captivating, and engaging spaces, even with limited resources.

Thoughtfully planned outdoor classrooms provide active play opportunities that are vital to young children's healthy development. Children thrive as they explore and engage in beautiful environments with natural elements. Inspiring outdoor learning spaces improve children's well-being, support learning and development, change behavior, and encourage healthy risk-taking. An effective outdoor environment, however, depends greatly on design and materials. Outdoor play yards come in a wide variety of shapes and sizes, with diverse circumstances that may be considered a delight or a barrier: size, ground coverings, permanent features, natural elements, storage, and resources. When design obstacles are viewed as opportunity rather than a challenge, many creative and favorable possibilities emerge.

Outdoor play zones for all ages of children follow the same principles, but aspects of the environment require different considerations. We adjust ground surfaces, equipment heights, and the size of the space to meet developmental needs. A smaller protected sand area is appropriate for infants and toddlers, while an expansive sand area is needed for the active play of preschoolers and school-aged children. Children can use the same loose parts according to their interests and abilities. An infant crawls up a wood plank propped on a tire. A toddler walks up the inclined plank and jumps off the tire to the grass below. A preschooler jumps from tire to tire. A school-aged child designs an elaborate obstacle course using tires and planks.

Reflected in this book are outdoor design ideas geared for young children ages zero to five, although the design ideas are suitable for school-aged children as well. In fact, two of my recent memories involve school-aged children's active engagement with transformed environments. The first incident occurred at an open house for a renovated family child care outdoor environment. Older siblings of children attending the program were captivated all afternoon. Their sustained engagement and actions with sand and the mud kitchen were a delight to watch. The second incident happened as I finished transforming a toddler yard on a rural elementary school campus. The school is a one-room classroom consisting of kindergarten through third grade students. The older children kept peeking at our construction work throughout the installation day but were redirected by their teachers to other areas of the play yard. Upon completion of the yard, I invited the children to come check it out. They were immediately enthralled with the trajectory wall, where objects or water can slide down ramps and through tubing, and with the sand area. These students are lucky, as they will have access to the play zones during their outdoor time.

Design ideas appropriate for both center- and home-based environments are included in this book. Outdoor play zones are the same for each program type, but various aspects of the environment require different considerations. Creating outdoor spaces in family child care programs, for example, requires thought concerning home and child care usage needs. Space may be limited in home programs, or providers may want to maintain adult spaces when children are not present. Many of the book's images are taken in family child care environments. Hopefully the photos will inspire you to create distinctive spaces, whether at a home- or center-based program.

This book invites you to reimagine and reconstruct your image of conventional play yards and create beautiful outdoor learning spaces on a limited budget, using natural elements and loose parts that offer children opportunities for irresistible engaging explorations. Join me on a journey to transform outdoor play environments as I share ideas, inspiration, and benefits for changing your own outdoor environment. Learn the basics for designing, transforming, and maintaining specific outdoor play zones.

First, I want to be transparent and disclose that I am not a landscape or playground architect. I am a retired early childhood college professor with many years of practical experience as a classroom educator and administrator in preschool, parent cooperative, and college lab settings. I know children, development, and learning well. I can spot what children find fascinating, and I know how to set up spaces to support and extend their interests. Recently I have been mentoring educators in transforming their thinking and environments. During mentoring sessions, I use an approach that results in amazing transformation of play yards, educator thinking, and children's behavior, learning, and play opportunities. Many educators have asked about this process. I am happy to share my joy and design plan for transforming outdoor environments with you here.

Chapter Organization

Chapters are organized according to play zones, selected because of their potential to encourage schema learning (repeating patterns in children's play), play themes, and developmentally appropriate learning. Zones can be clustered into creative (art studios, clay studios, sound gardens), imaginative (mud kitchens and small worlds), active (construction, trajectory, and large motor), sensory (sand and water), and quiet (cozy areas):

Art studio: a space for children to do art outside, such as drawing or painting on surfaces with different media and designing, modeling, or transforming materials in new ways

Clay studio: a space for children to express their energy, creativity, emotions, and ideas as they manipulate natural clay

Sound garden: a space for sound exploration, using upcycled materials such as pots and pans for children to explore pitch, dynamics, tempo, and rhythm

Mud kitchen: sometimes referred to as an outdoor kitchen, a space designed for children to pretend to cook, mix concoctions, experiment, and transform

Small world: imaginative play experiences in miniature, similar to a fairy garden or dollhouse; playscapes that promote dramatic play and expand children's imaginations

Construction zone: a space for building real and imaginary structures on a larger scale than indoors

Trajectory zone: an area to explore moving objects, featured as a trajectory wall with inclines secured to a vertical surface or offered in other zones such as sand and water

Large-motor zone: a space with large loose parts, such as tires, crates, planks, and ladders, that provides an alternative to fixed play equipment

Sand zone: a spacious area of sand for children to dig, tunnel, trench, excavate, dump, and make sandcastles and mud pies

Water zone: a sensory play area for children to freely explore the physical properties of water with a wide variety of containers, tools, and loose parts

Cozy spaces and hiding places: protected, peaceful, and safe refuges for children to have solitude, relax, or self-regulate, alone or with a friend

Value of the Zone

Each chapter begins with a vignette story followed by an introduction to the value of the zone for children's development.

Schema Learning

In each chapter you will discover ways that common action schemas are spotted in the play zone. I encourage you to intentionally look for these behaviors and implement the ideas to enhance schema learning. It is important to look for patterns in behavior and not just isolated incidents. Be creative in discovering additional ways and opportunities for children to explore schemas.

Fostering Learning in the Zone

Highlighting stories of children at play, this section covers how play in the area fosters children's competencies, development, and learning in social and emotional, language and communication, cognitive, physical, and expressive arts domains.

Essential Components

Practical guidance is provided on the important elements that the zone needs so it will be an engaging and effective play space. There are considerations for zone location, work space, furnishings and materials, loose parts, storage and organization, and cleaning and maintaining the area. Advice is given about ground surfaces, functionality, setup, and special touches to enhance and beautify the space.

Before and After Photos

In each chapter, a before photo of how a zone looked is highlighted alongside a photo taken after a transformation. The before photos demonstrate how a space can be changed for function, organization, and aesthetic appeal with minimal resources. The after photos illustrate creative ideas for designing stunning and captivating play spaces.

Top Tips for Designing the Zone

There is nothing more satisfying than creating a play zone that is beautiful, engaging, organized, and functional, but doing so takes time, hard work, and thoughtfulness. Detailed suggestions for designing each zone are found within the chapter text; however, for those of you who are impatient and like a quick, concise how-to guide, check out the top tips list offered with the "after" photos.

Tools and Materials

This section includes a list of tools and loose parts that are particularly good for the zone, but please feel free to add your own loose parts ideas. Storage ideas for accessibility, simplicity, and organization are included. Maintenance suggestions highlight ways to ensure safety, cleanliness, and usage.

Images

Rich, vivid photographs illustrate how chapter concepts look in real programs. There are design variations from center-based and home-based early care and education programs, as well as images of how concepts are applied in large and small spaces. Also included are photos of materials, accessories, storage options, organization systems, and children engaged in each zone. I am a visual learner and find that images trigger my creativity and make it easier for me to understand concepts. My hope is that the photographs provide you with inspiration and ideas for creating play spaces with upcycled materials that are captivating, aesthetically beautiful, and engaging.

The Extra Dimension

In this section, a unique idea for adding to the play zone is offered. This is a little something extra that will enrich the play space for children. It may be a creative idea, an unusual furnishing, or a way to make the space more visually appealing.

Supporting Equitable Learning

Adaptations and supports are included to ensure that all children are included as successful, engaged learners in the space. To design a play zone that works for every child, consideration must be given for children with a variety of abilities, languages, cultures, and experiences, as well as ages and sizes.

Adaptations for Infants and Toddlers

Mobile infants and toddlers can engage in all play zones if materials are suitable, safe, and accessible. Tips are provided for adapting play zones so infants and toddlers can freely explore developmentally appropriate materials safely and securely.

Appendices

Appendix A gives an example of the Be, Do, Become process discussed in chapter 1. Appendix B provides a rubric for assessing your current outdoor environment and planning your future transformation. Appendix C is a complete list of the materials, nature materials, and loose parts suggested in the book, organized by chapter. Appendices are available starting on page 239 or by scanning the QR codes on pages 21, 22, and 26.

Beginning the Transformation Journey

Outdoor learning environments should be designed with the same intentionality as indoor learning environments. With creativity and determination, all indoor play zones can be set up outdoors. Furthermore, bringing inside play experiences outdoors can generate new interest and play prospects. Imagine the joy that a child experiences when allowed to freely explore and transform an outdoor environment into whatever they desire, individually or with friends. I recommend that you begin by reading the first chapter, which unpacks the what, why, and how of transforming outdoor learning environments. Then dive into play zone chapters for ideas, inspiration, and benefits, and to learn designing, transforming, and maintenance strategies. May you be encouraged and inspired on your journey to transform captivating outdoor learning environments for young children.

Chapter 1
The What, Why, and How of Transforming Outdoor Learning Environments

Early Head Start funding afforded Maggie the opportunity to receive mentoring while transforming her family child care program into a loose parts play environment. Initially, Maggie and her husband, Randy, wanted to preserve a large portion of their backyard as an adult space without evidence of child care. Throughout the weeks of mentoring and participating in the outdoor transformation process, including a field trip to see the expansive, natural, and captivating environment of another home-based program, Maggie and Randy realized that child care, beauty, and personal space can coexist. With their growing knowledge of the loose parts philosophy and the importance of natural environments, they were willing to commit their entire outdoor area to children's play. The result was a visually appealing, engaging, natural environment. Today the two enjoy morning coffee and evening dinners in their beautiful yard while children delight in the inspiring environment during the day.

What Is *Transforming Your Outdoor Early Learning Environment*?

Dreaming about captivating learning spaces in your outdoor environment is exciting, but knowing where to begin or what to do to enhance your space can be challenging and confusing. Following a comprehensive, practical, and effective process will clarify your vision, affirm your values, and direct you in planning an environment with elements that positively affect the children who use them. The what, why, and how components provided here reveal the essential beliefs that serve as the foundation for transforming outdoor play spaces and are intended to guide you from project inception to installation.

The *Transforming Your Outdoor Early Learning Environment* approach is one that does the following:

Requires minimal resources: Many early childhood programs survive on limited operating funding. Often most startup funds are delegated to materials and equipment for the interior environment, leaving little or no resources for outdoor play spaces. The good news is that money is not necessarily a barrier. Engaging outdoor play zones may be created with imagination, effort, knowledge of community resources, volunteer help, and minimal cash.

Features loose parts: Loose parts are fundamental materials for every outdoor play zone. Their availability, versatility, economic feasibility, sustainability, and attractiveness make them the perfect open-ended items for children's play. The undefined nature of loose parts allows for maximum creative use in children's play.

Uses upcycled materials: Sustainability is one of the biggest challenges that currently faces our planet. Educating the next generation to be good stewards and being one yourself are top priorities. One way to help children learn about their impact on the environment is through the reuse of materials. Finding discarded items and repurposing them to create new play possibilities is a central component of the framework.

Integrates nature: Many children today live in neighborhoods surrounded by asphalt and concrete and have little connection with nature. Contact with nature contributes to the health and well-being of children (Chawla 2015). Adding natural materials such as plants, rocks, and tree trunks gives texture to play surfaces, enhances outdoor play spaces, and connects children and nature. Tree trunks are cut sections of the large central part

of a tree. At 12 to 24 inches in width, they sit on end and can range up to 18 inches in height. They are wide enough for children to walk, climb, balance, and sit on.

Emphasizes aesthetics and authenticity: Beauty is a fundamental component of outdoor play spaces. Environments affect how we feel, think, and behave. Surrounding children and educators with art, natural materials, and interesting textures, colors, and sounds enhances the beauty of play spaces. Authentic materials offer an aesthetic attractiveness while providing meaning and relevance to children's play. Children often prefer to engage with real cooking, art, or gardening tools used by adults rather than play imitations. Generally, real materials are appealing, of greater quality, and more durable. They often work better and are more effective and reliable.

For children, *Transforming Your Outdoor Early Learning Environment* is an approach that does the following:

Recognizes outdoor play as central to whole-child learning and development: Thoughtfully designed outdoor learning environments support children's growth and development across the emotional, social, physical, cognitive, and creative domains. Children are capable and competent learners and are the most important individuals in their own learning and development. Giving children many varied outdoor experiences and opportunities supports and challenges their whole learning and development.

Incorporates opportunities for open-ended exploration and active learning: Children learn best through experiential, active learning opportunities. Child-initiated outdoor explorations including loose parts foster creativity, self-discovery, self-direction, self-evaluation, expression of feelings, and freedom of choice. Active learning means the following:

- Children control materials rather than the materials controlling the child.

- Children decide what they are going to do with the materials and how they are going to use them.

- Children can use materials in multiple ways.

Offers intriguing and captivating play spaces: Rich, intriguing environments offer children opportunities for risk-taking, inquiry, wonder, innovation, and imagination. The complexity of the landscape affords a variety of play activities.

Supports equitable learning: Children of all ages, stages, temperaments, learning modalities, and abilities can successfully engage in rich, in-depth outdoor experiences. The open-ended nature of loose parts and flexible spaces accommodates all children.

Offers opportunities for meaningful connections: Intentional outdoor spaces and experiences are designed for collaboration. The availability, type, and location of loose parts along with space layout offer possibilities for children to connect with others and build strong relationships.

For educators, *Transforming Your Outdoor Early Learning Environment* is an approach that:

Incorporates a design process based on inquiry: An open-ended method to design is guided by reflection, assessment, and analysis. Involvement in the process creates more innovative, collaborative, and thoughtful designs that reflect the ideas and vision of all who participate. Time spent planning up front will eliminate potential challenges in the future.

Provides an action plan: An overall master plan offers a big-picture look at the outdoor play zones. A plan keeps the transformation on track and provides a guide for implementing the process in the most effective way. Whether the design is carried out all at once or broken down into phases and installed over an extended time as finances, time, and energy allow, a master plan ensures continuity.

Involves imagination, creativity, and satisfaction: Finding sources of inspiration, upcycling items in innovative ways, discovering solutions to problems, collaborating with others, and engaging in hard work all bring immense joy and satisfaction. Transforming unattractive and underused parts of the play yard into beautiful and captivating play spaces is exciting, particularly when you see children's delight and engagement.

Focuses on connections and community: Participating in a reflective and collaborative process builds connections. It is very satisfying to actively participate in the design and construction phases and know that your ideas and help are valued. Relationships are strengthened as teachers, family members, and friends work alongside each other. Community partnerships develop as materials are purchased and donated from local sources. Environments are designed to reflect the natural features in the community, such as rock and wood native to the area, bringing a sense of community and familiarity to children and families.

The Why of *Transforming Your Outdoor Early Learning Environment*

After a scenic drive through magnificent coastal redwoods and spectacular segments of the California coast, my friend Cheri and I met Nina, a family child care provider in Humboldt County. Nina had previously attended one of our presentations on transforming outdoor environments with loose parts, and she was excited to tell us her story. After learning about loose parts, Nina removed the gray plastic climbing castle from the large-motor area in her yard and replaced it with large, open-ended loose parts—tires, planks, and tree trunks. At one point, she even added a mini trampoline. Nina told us how transformation in the children's skill and ability levels was immediate. Previously, children simply ran around in the area, ignoring the climbing castle. After adding the large materials, play in the space dramatically changed. She witnessed increased muscle strength, balance, communication, risk-taking, problem solving, creativity, and collaboration when the children were in control of designing and changing the loose parts. Nina observed more growth in a few short hours than she had seen over a year. Creating new learning spaces from unused, uninteresting, and unattractive areas in a play yard supports loose parts play, schema learning, and common outdoor play themes in addition to fostering children's learning and development.

Nina instinctively recognized the value of loose parts over fixed play equipment in a play yard. Outdoor play environments composed of loose parts afford children opportunity to imagine, discover, and create in ways that do not happen with fixed play yard equipment. Regular play yards start to feel rather sterile, while play yards filled with loose parts change as children's interests and competencies evolve. While there are advantages to fixed play equipment, play with loose parts offers a richer learning environment.

Play Yard Comparison

Fixed Equipment	Loose Parts
Expensive to purchase and can be expensive to install.	Inexpensive or free; sustainable.
Needs weekly inspections to look for use, weathering, and vandalism on the structure and protective ground surfacing; needs quarterly inspections of equipment and surfaces for wear and tear. May need to replace hardware.	Require some maintenance. Some resources need to be washed and cleaned. For example, mud kitchen utensils need to be hosed off periodically. Need to be assessed for appropriateness prior to placing in the environment. Need to be checked before and during play sessions to remove any hazards. For example, splintered wooden planks need sanding.
Requires no additional labor other than replacing broken, cracked, loose, missing, rusted pieces if needed.	Must be initially gathered and collected by educators or donated by parents and the community. Must be replenished as they wear out.
Requires close supervision, particularly near swings, slides, and climbers, where most playground injuries result (Sawyers 1994).	Invite educators to stand back, observe, and allow children to lead their play.
Requires no storage.	Require storage such as containers, shelving units, or sheds that children may independently access. Invite children to participate in cleanup routine.
Is static and intended to be used in specific ways.	Create richer play environments for children. Allow children to redesign the environment as frequently as desired.
Benefits gross-motor play (climbing, jumping, spinning, sliding).	Accommodate all play types equally (creative, imaginative, social, physical, and cognitive).
May not be inclusive or accessible for all children.	Are inclusive of all children.
Is less flexible to children's ideas.	Allow all children to create, imagine, explore, transform, and more to make their ideas real in the world.
Becomes boring over time.	Become more engaging over time as children's skills increase.
Provides opportunity for social interaction.	Foster high levels of peer play and social unity.

Suzanna Law and Morgan Leichter-Saxby offer a comparison that illustrates benefits of loose parts play yards over yards composed of traditional, fixed equipment (2015). I encourage you to compare features of both play yard options to determine for yourself which approach offers deeper learning opportunities for children.

Supporting Schema Learning: It's Not about Purple

A key reason for creating well-designed outdoor spaces is to respond to and support children's intent. Observing for children's fascinations, focus, persistence, and resolve will guide you in creating intriguing spaces and provisioning them with loose parts that support and extend children's interests. Careful observation of children at play will reveal specific recurring interests or behaviors called *schemas*. Schema learning is a theory about how children learn and think: "A schema is a thread of thought which is demonstrated by repeated actions and patterns in children's play or art" (Wijk 2008, 1). Young children learn and form cognitive structures in their minds through schema learning. Action schemas are one type of schema; they focus on ideas about movement in the physical world. Action schemas are typically easy to identify, so they are a good way to begin schema recognition in the outdoors. Characteristics of children engaged in schema play include intense concentration, persistence, complete absorption, a sense of wonder, and deep enjoyment and satisfaction. Once adults notice schemas in young children's play, they can respond in ways that extend and support children's learning.

One of the most helpful ways I have found to discover children's interests is to pursue the action, rather than the object with which the child is playing. Follow the verb rather than the noun. While visiting a practicum student, I observed the student attentively watching a four-year-old girl make circles with a purple crayon on round paper attached to a lazy Susan. The child was skilled at placing the crayon tip securely on the paper and spinning the base while holding the crayon on the paper. She swiftly spun the lazy Susan round and round and round. For several minutes, the girl remained focused and persevered with the spinning action. When the child finished, I asked the student what she noticed about that moment. Totally missing the point, she replied, "She likes the color purple." It was not about purple or the crayon (nouns) but the rotating action (verb). The girl had a fascination with rotating schema. When you practice following children's actions, you will get really good at identifying their intent. Once you have observed multiple occurrences of the same action, you can determine ways to support and extend children's interests. Here are some examples of focusing on the action.

Things or Actions

Noun = Thing	Verb = Action
Ball	rolling, accelerating, racing, cascading, falling, speeding, throwing, bouncing, tossing, tumbling, dropping, propelling, flinging
Scarf	spinning, twirling, rotating, revolving, whirling, spiraling, turning, twisting, wrapping, covering
Rope	connecting, joining, tying, attaching, hooking, securing, fastening, fixing, binding
Clay	pounding, pinching, squishing, squeezing, rolling, digging, shredding, crushing, hitting, tearing, flattening, stretching, poking, pulling, pushing

Here is a list of what to look for in action schemas that are commonly seen in children's play. Know that spotting a behavior pattern and supporting a child's interest is more important than discerning which schema is happening.

Transporting: Children with an interest in transporting like to move objects from one place to another. They may transport containers of water to the sand area or push a dump truck loaded with dirt or collect a bucket of natural materials. Transporters may also be interested in putting things in their pockets or being transported themselves, such as riding in a wagon. Loose parts particularly good for transporters include all kinds of containers and materials to move from one place to another.

Transforming: Children with a fascination for transforming like to change things to see what happens. They may add water to dirt, mix paint colors, or reshape clay. Dressing up and changing appearance, combining vinegar and baking soda, and rearranging materials to create new spaces are exciting experiences for transformers. Malleable loose parts that are especially good for transformers include paint, sand, water, and clay. Design materials, textiles, and blocks are also good options.

Trajectory: Children who are captivated with trajectory like things that move through space. They may throw or kick objects, roll balls down inclines, or pour water into funnels or rain gutters. Their own bodies may be the trajectory object as they jump off high places, swing, or roll down hills. Loose parts that support an interest in trajectory include inclines and a variety of objects that roll.

Rotation: Children who gravitate toward objects that spin or roll have an interest in rotating schema. They may love to spin on a tire swing, participate in salad spinner art, or spin tops. You may observe children drawing circles, rolling hoops and balls, or watching wheels go round and round. Loose parts that foster children's interest in rotation include materials that are round or that spin.

Enclosing and enveloping: Children who are attracted to making boundaries around things find enclosing appealing. They may use blocks to enclose space that may be referred to as a house, garage, or zoo. Children may also show an interest in enclosing if they paint a large shape and then fill in the shape's interior. Children who like covering and wrapping things may be attracted to enveloping. They may get inside hiding places, such as a cardboard box, industrial pipe, or blanket fort. Wrapping up a baby doll or covering up oneself with a blanket are favorite activities of envelopers. Loose parts for supporting an interest in enclosing and enveloping include textiles and construction materials.

Connecting and disconnecting: A fascination with connecting involves joining things together, while being drawn to taking things apart focuses on disconnecting. Children who like to connect may use rope or string to attach items and tie things up. They may also connect pipes or hoses. Children who are disconnectors like to take apart and scatter materials, knocking down block structures, breaking sticks into pieces, or smashing sandcastles. Loose parts that foster children's interest in connecting and disconnecting include rope, string, clay, sand, and pipes that connect.

Supporting Play Themes

Children engage in a variety of common outdoor play themes, and once you know these themes you can create interesting spaces and provision the environment with loose parts to strengthen, support, and extend children's interests and learning. Jan White proposed the following framework of children's play themes based on her research and work with children (Casey and Robertson 2019).

Adventure: Pursuing adventure, stretching boundaries, discovering, risking, taking chances, anticipating, venturing, and innovating. Loose parts afford children unlimited possibilities to undertake adventure, whether it be building tall or creating climbing structures.

Enclosure, dens, and special places: Making private, hiding, quiet, and secret places. This play theme relates to enclosing schema. Loose parts of planks, crates, and textiles present children with opportunities to design hiding spaces.

Prospect (height): Surveying pursuits, seeking high places, views, and lookouts, assessing the landscape, and making maps. Elements in the environment such as boulders or trees to climb, planks to balance on, or a dirt hill to scale all further children's quest for high places.

Paths and journeys: Exploring ways to travel across areas, investigating tunnels, discovering shortcuts and secret passages. Meandering pathways created from pavers, stones, and wood planks with bridges, vine-covered archways, and tunnels welcome children to travel to unknown places.

Hunter-gatherer activities: Searching, collecting, tracking, discovering, pursuing, gathering, hiding, stashing, storing, saving, and hoarding. This play theme is associated with transporting schema. A wide variety of containers and natural loose parts offer children opportunity to satisfy their desire to find and collect.

Animal allies: Caring for plants and animals, connecting to nature and wildlife. Gardening spaces allow children to grow and harvest food. Composting spaces let children experience the responsibility of caring for our environment. Animal spaces such as chickens in a chicken coop, bird-feeding stations, or insects in a bug hotel offer children opportunity to watch, care for, connect, and protect living things.

Imaginative narratives (stories, imagination, and fantasy): Making sense of the world through fantasy narratives, small-world play, and experiences that deepen friendships and relationships. Loose parts for storytelling and fantasy play along with small-world options support children's imaginative endeavors.

How to Transform Outdoor Learning Environments: A Framework

Transforming your outdoor environment may seem intimidating and challenging. You may feel overwhelmed and not know where to begin. You may lack vision or inspiration. Know that it is possible to transform any outdoor space into a beautiful and captivating learning environment, no matter the shape or size, with a thoughtful planning process. Following a framework can help you generate ideas, consider alternatives, identify considerations and resources, and ensure the overall success of your transformation. Framework phases include reflection, information collection, brainstorming and analysis, design development, action, and project construction.

Reflection Phase

One time as I was visiting Roseville Community Preschool, Bev Bos told me a story of a family who was visiting their program to decide whether to enroll their son. As the mother and father struggled to get their child to leave the play yard, the boy resisted and replied, "Leave me here!" His words reflected his innate awareness of the environment and the strong sense of safety, security, and adventure he felt there. When we enter a space, we are influenced by what we see and hear, and we receive implicit messages about what to expect and how to behave. An outdoor environment can encourage children to explore, take risks, connect, create, and be independent. The physical arrangement of materials, equipment, and space suggests what happens in the area. For example, a wide-open space says, "Run and shout." Materials on low, accessible shelves promote independence. A cozy, private space invites children to relax and get away from the busy outdoor environment. Loose parts encourage children to use materials as they desire rather than in a designed way.

Transforming your space begins by participating in a "be, do, and become" reflective process. Reflect on who children are in outdoor spaces, how they currently use the spaces, and what they become or gain through play in these spaces. Use your understanding of children's development, learning, and developmentally appropriate practices to guide your reflections. I was introduced to this process by early childhood educators from the Children's Center at the University of California, Santa Barbara, who used the format when designing their outdoor play environment. The three-step progression of thought is revealing and helpful for designing outdoor or indoor play zones. Brainstorm (as a teaching staff if you work with others) a list of characteristics and actions you have observed in children as they engage in the outdoor environment. Start with the word *be*, followed by *do*, and then *become*. Record the identified words on chart paper. After completing this exercise, it is helpful to keep the words posted in an accessible space for an extended time so that words may be added.

Be: Who are children in the outdoors? For example, a child may be curious, creative, energetic, or messy. If you are stuck with this step, try working backward from actions you observe. For example, if I jump, I may be fearful or courageous. If I see something new, I may be excited or uncertain.

Do: What do children do in the space? These are the actions that children engage in, such as dumping, filling, spinning, climbing, and designing.

Become: What do children become as they play outdoors? For example, children may become confident, capable, strong, and compassionate through their actions.

Appendix A documents the Be, Do, Become process of an outdoor planning session with educators at Creative Spirit Learning Center in Fair Oaks, California.

For educators, the reflective phase is a time to consider what is working for you and what is not. The idea is to design spaces that promote independence, competency, discovery, risk, collaboration, and engagement for children. A thoughtfully designed space will allow more time for you to engage in meaningful observations, interactions, and conversations with children. Specific considerations for each play zone are provided in respective chapters, but here are a few questions to reflect on to enhance your current outdoor space:

www.redleafpress
.org/toe/a-1.pdf

- What loose parts and real tools can be added to each play zone?

- What materials and resources can be available for children to move around, modify their environment, and decide their use?

- How can adequate storage space be created in each zone so that materials may stay outdoors and not have to be hauled in and out each day?

- How can materials be organized in a visible way so that children can independently access them and take them back without adult assistance?

- Where are the spaces for sensory exploration, constructing, creating, transforming, surveying, traversing, transporting, nurturing, and imagining?

- How can natural elements for exploring be incorporated in the environment?

- How can spaces be designed for convenience and easy cleanup?

- How can the play environment provide opportunities for children to gain competence and experience appropriate challenges?

- How are areas designed for ease of supervision?

- How can spaces for your comfort be created by including a bench, log, chair, or similar item to sit on?

- How can the space welcome families and provide a sense of belonging?

- How can spaces be created for families to connect and share?

- How can spaces be created for families to sit, hang out, and watch their child play?

- How can spaces be designed that reflect the lives, cultures, and interests of families in your program?

Information Collection Phase

www.redleafpress
.org/toe/a-2.pdf

Assess the environment by exploring and investigating the current yard. It can be helpful to use a chart of outdoor play zones and record what is already present to support children's interests and ideas in the zone and what you would like to see. Appendix B: Assessing Your Current Outdoor Environment can be used as a guide. Often this step involves program educators, but it can include perspectives from children and families who use the play space. Selim Iltus and Roger Hart address the importance of transparency, feedback, and negotiation when children participate in the design process (1995). This recommendation also applies to families and educators. If you decide to involve children and families, asking specific questions to solicit perspectives is not enough. Token involvement does not help individuals develop competence in planning, designing, negotiating, and problem solving. Authentic participation, problem identification, shared decision-making, and discourse need to be transparent throughout the whole process for all involved participants.

Observing other programs is an excellent way to generate design ideas. It has been my experience that early childhood educators are very receptive to giving program tours, sharing ideas, and offering valuable insight. You may discover solutions to design challenges, organizational strategies, new-found materials, or an intriguing way to set up a space. You may discover things that would *not* work for you, which is also helpful in identifying your vision. I prefer observing while children are present to see how they engage in the environment. Sometimes a space may seem too risky, noisy, or messy for your comfort, but your mind may be put at ease once you see how children use the materials. You will come away from program visitations feeling motivated, inspired, and encouraged.

Starting a gallery of inspirational photos can be another invaluable tool. As you discover photos of intriguing spaces and materials on image sharing and social media venues, save a copy and begin an inspiration board. Photos from program visitations and other places of inspiration can also be added. I frequently take photos of store displays, natural elements, and architectural elements that I find interesting when I am out and about. The intent is not to replicate exactly what you saw but rather to spark creativity, help you identify and refine important elements, and provide clear direction.

Brainstorming and Analysis Phase

Now it is time to share and discuss the reflections and information that you have gathered. Refer to your discoveries about commonly seen characteristics, actions, and interests you observed in children as they used spaces. Consider the responses to guiding questions and other information you collected. What constraints need to be considered? What possibilities are there? Identify goals, priorities, uses for space, wishes, limitations, and resources. Formulate ideas about how best to design the outdoors. For example, if information gathering reveals children are intrigued with trajectory, design spaces to support their interest. If keeping areas flexible is a goal, create spaces with movable furnishings and loose parts. If a sand area is a priority, determine where it will go first. Concrete ground surfaces work well for multiple play zones, so thought is needed to determine which zone provides the best use of space. Will an art studio or construction area be the best choice? You may desire a hand water pump for the sand area, but lack of resources requires that it remain on the wish list. Limited space requires creative ways to ensure large-motor experiences. A sound garden may need to be located away from a neighbor's home.

Beginning your transformation with a clearly defined plan and scope of design is critical to the success of the project. Time spent designing and planning will uncover potential problems and result in fewer costly mistakes. During the design development phase, you will gain a clear perspective of the overall environment layout by creating a sketch, a scaled drawing, and finally a schematic of the design to help you visualize the plan and see the big picture.

Photograph the space: Take "before" photos to document what the yard looks like before the transformation. The photos will be a helpful reference throughout the drawing and design phases. Sometimes sketches are confusing and a photo can provide clarity. It is also immensely powerful to look back at the existing space at the end of a project and see the incredible transformation.

Sketch the space: Draw a rough sketch of the play yard on paper. Start with a basic outline of the overall shape of the space, followed by large permanent features, and then move to specific elements. Include existing fixed and natural features, including permanent structures, sandboxes, pathways, trees, boulders, garden areas, and fences. Also identify ground surfaces and note the location of water sources, gates, stairs, and building doors and windows that may affect the design.

Record measurements: After your sketch is complete, it is time to record measurements. It is helpful to have two people assist with measuring. A contractor's measuring wheel is a handy tool to quickly maneuver and measure long distances. One person can measure and call out the numbers while the second person helps and records the measurements on the sketch. Begin by recording the length and width of play space. Record the overall dimensions of each space. To get exact placement of fixed features, measure distances from at least two different points of reference. For example, measure the location of a tree from a fence line and a pathway. Be certain to clearly record beginning and ending points of each dimension on your sketch. Use a line with small perpendicular marks on its ends to show what the measurement represents. Take time to double-check measurements and make certain that all details are included on the sketch.

Convert the sketch to a scaled drawing: Once you have added all the measurements to your rough sketch, it is time to draw your sketch to scale. I find it helpful to transfer the sketch onto graph paper so the squares serve as the measuring unit. Use "1 square equals 1 foot" scale on graph paper for simplicity, or 1 square for 2 feet for large play yards. Make the plan as big as possible, being certain that the space fits on the paper with space to spare along the edges. Then, beginning with the outdoor perimeter, start drawing elements in proportion with pencil. Add in doors, gates, windows, and other built-in features.

Create a design schematic: Now that you have a sketch to scale, it is time to create a preliminary design by organizing and defining locations of play zones. I typically make a few copies of the sketch so I can play with different zone locations and see which option works best. Each play zone chapter in this book contains information about location considerations, including sun, shade, ground cover, and amount of space, and whether the zone is quiet, noisy, active, or messy. A general rule is to begin with fixed features that cannot be changed. I often determine where water sources are first and locate water and sand areas near them if possible. Now is the time to be creative and develop a plan with colleagues. Use reflections, brainstorming sessions, and inspiration photos to decide the best usage of space. Refine the preliminary design into a final schematic. Consider making a colorful computer rendering of the schematic, or find a family member, colleague, or friend who is willing to help if you don't have the software or technical skills yourself.

Develop a budget: An important part of the design phase is developing a budget. Now that your design is complete, play zone locations, size, and ground coverings have been finalized. You are ready to calculate material quantities and receive pricing. Employees at landscape companies are extremely helpful in determining cubic yards of material needed based on the length, width, and depth of the space. Remember to factor in delivery fees.

A friendly warning: While it is important to have an overall design plan, I want to emphasize that the plan will change during installation. Most often these changes end up being better than the original plan. Borders or boundaries may change because of the shape and size of found tree trunks. As an area is created, more or less space may be necessary. A material or piece of furniture may not be available. Someone may find a unique element while collecting materials or come up with an irresistible new idea. I encourage you to be flexible and embrace these changes. The result will be magnificent.

Action Phase

The action phase includes developing a plan to begin the play yard transformation. An established action plan will make for a successful project. Work to be done is identified and a timeline drawn up. It may be that you

www.redleafpress
.org/toe/a-3.pdf

decide to complete the entire outdoor transformation at once or divide the project into manageable stages as time and resources allow.

Make a list of ground covers, furniture, fixtures, accessories, and materials for each play zone. You will find suggestions for these items specific to each play zone in each chapter. Appendix C: Outdoor Zone Materials and Accessories includes loose parts suggestions for various play zones. Once materials and donations are identified, they may be collected or purchased and scheduled for delivery.

Finding and collecting loose parts for play zones is exciting and immense fun, and I and many others find it addictive. Loose parts are everywhere, so always be on the lookout. Natural loose parts such as seedpods, leaves, and rocks may be found in your home yard, neighborhood, and community, and in nature at a beach, desert, mountain, or lake. Gathering a few natural objects found on the ground, such as pine cones and dead wood, for personal use may be permitted at some state parks, but you should check local regulations. Get children involved—remember that gathering and transporting are favorite activities. Garage sales and thrift stores are economical places to find pots, pans, and kitchen utensils. Home improvement stores and donation centers selling new and gently used furniture, home goods, building materials, and surplus items are perfect places to secure items that can be repurposed for play. Free loose parts can be found from cabinet makers (wood scraps), tree trimmers (tree trunks), and appliance stores (cardboard cove molding). Research the free or inexpensive resources in your local community, or ask other local educators for advice. Describe what loose parts are to neighbors, family members, and friends, and solicit their ideas and help collecting. You may be amazed by their contributions.

Determine the installation date(s) and prepare the site for transformation. Sometimes work needs to be completed prior to installation: moving a fence, removing a fixed climbing structure, or installing grass. It may be possible for some furniture, such as a mud kitchen or cozy area, to be constructed ahead of time. Organize materials and equipment according to play zones, and make certain that all crucial items are available. For example, you may need zip ties to secure a reed fence, paint supplies to stain a bridge, or screws to secure a trajectory track. Having materials at hand and accomplishing tasks early can save time later.

Project Construction Phase

Post information about the installation in a prominent place, and spread the word about the date as well as needed donations, equipment, and support well in advance. Displaying the color rendering of the plan can create anticipation. Solicit support from family members. Educators can talk about the project with family members during pickup and drop-off times and encourage them to sign up to help. Perhaps someone works as a tree trimmer and can begin to collect tree trunks. Perhaps somebody has rock, wood, or bricks on their property that they would like to donate. Often you will discover family members with expertise in specific areas such as carpentry or landscaping who are delighted to lend a hand. Most of the work requires no skill other than a willingness to show up and work hard. Work such as hauling sand and rock is labor intensive, so having people work in shifts is a good option. Some family members may not be able to commit to a full day but are more than willing to contribute a couple of hours of time. Provide a list of helpful items to bring, such as gloves, wheelbarrows, rakes, and shovels. For family members who cannot attend a work day, consider projects that can be done at home. Making pillows, repairing equipment, or cutting tree cookies (branch and log slices) are some options.

Welcome helpers by providing water, snacks, and lunch. Rich conversations and a sense of community occur while sharing food. Children show a sense of pride and ownership when they can share that their grandma painted the bridge or their dad made the sand area. Family members and staff connect with each other as they sand wood and put together furniture. Involving families and center staff in the installation is a way to build relationships, promote family engagement, and save costs and time. Participating in the installation is an in-kind activity for family members to record volunteer hours as part of any mandatory participation requirements. For families, volunteering with the play yard installation provides a sense of purpose, allows participants to learn new skills, and presents an opportunity to make friendships. Conversations about the shared experience will continue well after the installation. There is nothing more fulfilling for families than realizing how much of an impact volunteering can make on their child's education.

Outdoor Learning Environment Considerations

Whether indoors or outdoors, the environment needs to reflect the children and families who attend the program as well as the surrounding community and landscape, featuring local natural resources. Additionally, both environments need to include a full range of permanent play zones designed for independent use. For outdoors specifically, other factors, such as selecting materials that stand up to changing seasons and weather conditions and handling vandalism, need to be considered as part of the design process. It is likewise important to consider aesthetics, functionality, and cost effectiveness.

Feature Local Natural Resources

Having the play yard represent a community's landscape is an important aspect of its design. Natural elements from the area should dominate to provide a sense of belonging, familiarity, and community. The Early Years School in Santa Monica, California, is located three blocks from a sandy ocean beach. The play yard is filled with sand, driftwood, sea glass, and seashells from the local landscape. With rugged, rocky shores nearby, rocks and pebbles used as borders, landscaping, and loose parts bring these elements into the space.

Roong Aroon School in Bangkok, Thailand, is a community that values the natural environment. Its outdoor environments contain design elements that illustrate the essence of Bangkok culture, including water, earth, and wood, which represent calmness, tranquility, beauty, enrichment, and wonder. The preschool play yard is brilliantly landscaped with the natural beauty of a pond and creek, lush green trees and foliage, rocks, and art. Banyan trees for climbing are plentiful. Bamboo is found in brooms for sweeping and gutters for water play. Children can pump and spray water from the pond and rinse off feet at a water faucet. Meandering and challenging pathways are created with tree trunks, stones, and dark, rich wood. Sand is plentiful for digging and transforming. The entire school grounds are an excellent illustration of incorporating community.

Create Permanent Spaces

Just as inside, outdoor play zones are set up with materials that are attractively displayed, well organized, accessible, and available to children. Spaces are designed with a clear identity so that children know what happens in the area. In each play zone, children find all the materials needed for a specific kind of play, along with appropriate space to use them. For example, the large-motor area has loose parts such as tires, crates, tree trunks, wood planks, and ladders for building big structures for climbing and balancing. Children are free to move materials and redesign spaces as they desire.

Weather and Outdoor Materials

Some teachers report that being outside is not their favorite part of the day, as it takes a lot of time and energy to bring materials in and out from storage units or inside classrooms. One solution is to leave materials outside, planning ways to display them and protect them from excessive weathering. Rainy and snowy weather, hot and cold climates, and coastal air can all damage outdoor materials and furniture. Whether items will survive and maintain their beauty comes down to the materials. When assessing furniture, look for many of the same qualities that you value in indoor furniture, such as durability, accessibility, function, and design. The main difference, however, is that outdoor furniture and materials must withstand exposure to the weather. It is important to note that nothing is 100 percent weatherproof, but there are helpful factors to consider before investing time and money in outdoor materials.

Natural materials: Natural materials come from nature and are found outside. This makes them the perfect loose part for outdoors. It is okay for rocks, seashells, pine cones, leaves, and driftwood to get wet. Natural items can be added to yard debris or compost piles and be replaced as needed.

Outdoor patio furniture: Wooden outdoor patio furniture, such as benches, tables, wall panels, shelves, stools, and coffee tables, are good choices for storage units. Furniture treated with a water-based wood stain is durable enough for outdoor use. The life expectancy of wooden furniture depends on the climate and the furniture's exposure to sun, rain, and snow. Outdoor wood furniture does gray over time, so restaining with a waterproof stain and sealer once a year, or more frequently if necessary, prevents surfaces from drying out and cracking and keeps moisture from penetrating into the wood. If furniture is left exposed to rain or snow, protect it with a waterproof cover, such as a barbecue cover or tarp, and if possible, tilt the furniture to help water drain away. Keeping outdoor furniture under a solid roof such as a patio cover will also prolong use.

Stainless and galvanized steel: Stainless steel can withstand water and is resistant to corrosion due to an added chromium layer. Galvanized steel is coated in zinc, which makes it corrosion resistant too. Regular steel is made of iron, which will rust when exposed to moisture from rain or humidity. Aluminum is not a good choice. Even though it does not rust, it does corrode. Use containers that enhance the visual impact of materials. Shallow containers work well. If a container is too deep, children cannot see the materials within. Metal containers with open basket frames are preferred so that sand, dirt, and water fall through and do not collect at the bottom.

Textiles: Textiles can soften spaces and make areas feel cozy and welcoming. Many of today's outdoor fabrics are designed to withstand inclement weather, though they are not totally carefree. Anything that stays outside will collect dust or dirt and be subject to fading from the sun. The easiest and simplest solution for keeping outdoor cushions looking good is to cover them up or bring them inside when not in use. Consider covers that are removable and washable. Outdoor rugs can define and complement a desired space. Look for rugs that are made from materials such as bamboo or sisal, as they are typically low maintenance. However, even outdoor rugs need to be maintained and brought indoors during wet seasons.

Eliminate plastic: While items made from plastic may hold up well outdoors, most detract from rather than enhance the beauty of a natural environment (see the Aesthetics section on page 31). I encourage you to limit the inclusion of plastic materials.

Outdoor Maintenance

Outdoor play yards require regular maintenance just like a home yard. No yard is maintenance free. Throughout the year, things need to be painted, refinished, cleaned, repaired, cleared, and replaced to avoid expensive problems. A regular schedule of preventive maintenance is extremely helpful to ensure that everything is safe and in good repair.

Vandalism

Unfortunately, vandalism is a major concern for some early childhood programs. Willful destruction of property affects children, families, staff, and community, and it takes time and resources to replace materials and clean play yards. Similarly, some programs are located on school campuses that are frequented by older children who play with materials after school hours and may potentially damage them. These are legitimate concerns. Here are some suggestions for combating vandalism:

- Involve community members in designing and building the play yard. People are less likely to destroy property in which they have invested time, energy, and effort.

- Leave materials visible rather than locking them up. This may seem counterintuitive, but it has been my experience that closed and locked storage units invite unwelcome visitors to investigate. They are curious about what is inside the storage shed. Leaving materials out may take away the mystery. Old pieces of wood, gutters, and pots and pans are not that exciting.

- Lock entrances and exits.

- Keep areas well lit at night with security lights.

- Strategically plant shrubs and bushes around the yard's perimeter.

- Install video surveillance. The presence of cameras can be a deterrent. Some security systems allow you to get notifications when cameras detect motion and to watch live views from your cell phone.

- Involve young people in alternative school activities. Perhaps young people can paint a mural on the school building or work in a school garden.

- Secure costly items.

Aesthetics

Something that has aesthetic appeal is beautiful and attractive. Objects of aesthetic appreciation in an environment affect how children and adults feel and act in their surroundings. One change that makes the biggest difference in transforming a play yard's appearance is replacing plastic elements with natural ones. Think about a time when you hiked outdoors on a trail or along the beach. You appreciate the natural materials you see along the way, whereas a piece of plastic feels out of place. The same is true for a play yard. As your eye scans a yard, natural materials blend in, while a blue plastic shovel sticks out. Even if tree cookies are out of place, they are not a distraction. Begin by replacing plastic containers with metal ones and trading plastic shovels for abalone, scallop, and coconut shells.

I do make an exception and include black plastic storage crates in a play yard. I find that black crates blend into outdoor surroundings and are not distracting. Overall, however, I encourage you to eliminate plastic materials and replace them with natural ones to enhance a yard's visual appeal.

Natural elements: Enhance a yard's look by adding tree trunks as borders to sand areas or installing river rock to look like a creek bed. The natural colors of wood and river rocks make yard designs look spectacular. A rock strip around the school building, pathways edged with landscaping rocks, and rocks forming dry riverbeds add visual interest, texture, and contrast. Natural ground covers such as sand, gravel, cocoa mulch, and play bark become fodder for play as children use the loose materials for imagining and constructing. Installing natural reed garden fencing is an easy and inexpensive way to create privacy and natural beauty. It comes in rolls and can be attached to an existing fence. Bamboo rolls, fence panels, and screens are pricier but come in several options. Consider repurposing downed tree branches and logs and rocks. Pine cones, acorns, seedpods, and leaves can

further enhance aesthetics and play opportunities. Heighten the sensory allure of play materials with seasonal loose parts that are native to your area, such as grapevines, gourds, dried flowers, chestnuts, jacaranda pods, and evergreen needles.

Art elements: Enhance the beauty of outdoor spaces by placing attractive furnishings throughout the play yard. Outdoor décor using plants, textiles, and upcycled pieces in addition to sculptures and works of art, can totally transform how spaces feel. Position wall décor on fences or buildings to make outdoor areas more inviting. Bare walls can be covered with a trellis, latticework, pallets, shutters, or vertical gardens. Many planters are made to hang flat against a wall. Succulent or herb gardens in hollowed-out logs bring rustic texture to spaces. Children can make functional art, such as decorative stepping-stones for pathways or mosaics on terra-cotta flowerpots. Consider adding a little whimsy by hiding metal statues in foliage. Suspend wind chimes from tree branches or rafters. Children can help create colorful strands of glass beads to suspend from a piece of driftwood. Having art in the play yard not only adds visual appeal but helps children to see the world in new, exciting ways and gain an appreciation for art.

Functionality

Just as when designing a room in your home, space planning, layout, use, and storage are critical. How do you envision children will use each space? Refer to the reflection phase and the commonly seen characteristics, actions, and interests of children that you identified. After the function of each space has been defined, you can identify details of the design and materials. There is a difference between simply furnishing a play zone with materials and creating a space that offers functionality and identity. Each space should clearly convey what materials are available, include appropriate work space and storage, and have ample room to play. For example, if children will be pretending to cook, they need a standing work surface as well as strategically placed pots, pans, utensils, and dirt. There needs to be sufficient space, water access, and a ground surface that can get wet and muddy.

Storage: Incorporating adequate and well-placed storage in each zone is key to an organized and functional play space. Storage generally consists of simple shelving and containers. Here are some helpful strategies for maintaining organization:

- Create permanent, purposeful storage in each play zone.

- Use different surface levels.

- Store materials close to their intended use.

- Arrange materials on low, open, uncrowded shelves.

- Design storage for independent use.

- Position loose parts for easy accessibility.

- Present materials attractively.

- Display like materials together.

- Use attractive storage containers.

- Maintain organization; avoid clutter.

- Declutter on a regular basis.

- Offer a variety of diverse materials.

- Avoid displaying too many or too few materials.

Outdoor Storage Ideas

While nothing is 100 percent weatherproof, some materials hold up better than others. Here are some suggestions for storage-related items that endure exposure to weather outdoors:

STORAGE UNITS

bamboo shoe racks
commercial furniture made with weatherproof wood
metal shelves of stainless or galvanized steel
outdoor furniture made from hard wood such as teak, eucalyptus, redwood, or cedar
wood shelves painted with exterior paint
wooden crates
wrought iron furniture

CONTAINERS

metal baskets with open basket frames
stainless or galvanized steel

Accessibility: When arranging loose parts, think about how children will access them. Set up loose parts so children can see and reach objects. To make loose parts more accessible, place items on low shelves or in shallow open baskets and containers within children's reach. Arrange smaller items in front of taller ones so children can see what is available. Allow ample time for children to explore materials, and offer them opportunities to move items around the work space.

Simplicity: Display only one or two categories of materials at a time, and limit the number of containers. Two to four containers on a shelf is ideal. It is hard to find the right number of loose parts to display at a time. Too many items can be overwhelming and overstimulating for children, resulting in misuse of materials. Too few materials can frustrate children and limit their opportunities for play. This may cause conflicts among children trying to work with limited resources. One or two items are not enough to allow for rich explorations. Offering more of the same material allows for more complex play. For example, a provocation with large quantities of driftwood is stronger than a provocation with a few pieces each of driftwood, seashells, and stones.

Consistency and variety: Children deepen learning and understanding by repeating experiences and explorations. Familiarity with materials leads to competency and mastery of skills, techniques, tools, and media while discovering new possibilities. When children use the same materials, they make connections cognitively, physically, socially, and emotionally and also apply and expand established abilities and knowledge in new ways. For these reasons, it is helpful to keep a consistent supply of materials available at all times. Children also delight in surprises, however. The addition of a new tool or material or a change in the way in which items are displayed can pique interest and expand possibilities. For example, adding large sundial seashells with their magnificent spirals to a natural collection of materials may stimulate the creation of spiral designs. Children need both consistency and variety.

Cost Effectiveness

Budget, time, and space restraints are almost always an issue. There are, however, numerous economical ways to transform an outdoor play yard with limited resources. Upcycling materials, doing work yourself, buying in bulk, and using natural elements are all possible options.

Repurpose unwanted items: Expensive toys and playground equipment are not needed to construct interesting play spaces. Rain gutters or drain-pipes are great for flowing water or rolling balls, and they cost substantially less than productions from commercial play-based companies. A barrel may be upcycled into a cozy area or a sink into a small-world container. An entire sound garden may be created by suspending baking sheets and broiler pan racks in an open window frame. Take advantage of yard sales, online sites for reusing, reducing, and recycling, and thrift stores. Imagination and resourcefulness are all that is needed.

Save on labor costs: For the installation, do work yourself and solicit help from family volunteers. Providing meaningful opportunities for family involvement builds effective partnerships.

Buy in bulk: Purchase ground cover materials such as sand, gravel, stones, bark, and dirt in bulk from landscape suppliers. There will be a delivery fee, but it is still more economical than buying small prepackaged bags of items.

Secure tree trunks: Tree trunks and logs add natural beauty and make a big aesthetic impact in a play yard, but they can be hard to obtain. Make connections with a tree trimming service and also let family, neighbors,

and friends know that you need tree trunks. Watch for trees that have fallen in your neighborhood or community and ask permission from residents to keep the trunks for a children's play yard. I always store found trunks even if I do not have an immediate need. They need to be replaced periodically because of rot.

Find free natural resources: One of my favorite parts of teaching is finding free natural resources. In my own backyard I have what I refer to as future loose parts (that is, waiting to fall from the trees): liquid amber or sweetgum tree balls, pine needles, and large cones of Monterey pines. I always keep an extra bag or two in my car and pockets for collecting materials I discover while out and about. On walks around my neighborhood, I have found rose pine cones (deodar cedar tree), mini pine cones (shortleaf pine), and acorns. My walks to the lake yield fabulous pieces of driftwood. While driving, I have been known to stop and collect palm tree bark and eucalyptus bark and pods. At a family cabin, I have harvested large sugar pine cones (2 feet long!) and manzanita branches. Everywhere I travel, I make it my quest to discover a natural loose part native to the area.

Natural materials will vary according to your own geographic location. Always check regulations before collecting materials from local, state, and federal parks, as it may be forbidden or require a permit. For those of you who are not into collecting, natural loose parts are available for purchase on many internet sites and in craft stores.

Caution: Always make certain that any natural elements you find or purchase are not considered poisonous to humans or to pets, if they live in the environment.

Risk, Hazard, and Play

> "Everyday life always involves a degree of risk and children need to learn how to cope with this from an early age. They need to learn how to take calculated risks and, for this learning to happen, they need opportunities for challenging and adventurous play and to move and act freely."
> —Marie Willoughby (2011, 7)

Keeping children safe is a top priority, but imposing too many limitations on children's outdoor risky play can impede their development. Children need to see and experience the consequences of risk firsthand. Our role as early childhood educators is to understand the significance of risk in children's play and ensure a balanced, thoughtful approach between safety and risk. When children take risks, meet challenges, and experience adventure, they discover what they can do as well as the limits of their physical capabilities. A study by Ellen Beate Hansen Sandseter, Rasmus Kleppe, and Ole Johan Sando found that risky types of play are attractive to children and that given the opportunity to choose freely, children engage in this kind of play at the same level as other typical play types, such as symbolic play (2021). Joan Almon discusses the various kinds of risks that children should be allowed to take, such as scaling high climbing equipment or gliding on a zip line designed for children. She states that children have a natural capacity for risk assessment that needs to be cultivated and encouraged rather than inhibited (2013). Play is critical for children to acquire resiliency and risk management skills that will help them in adulthood.

First, it is important to distinguish the difference between a risk and a hazard, so play yards permit risk but remain safe and do not contain potential hazards. According to Fran Wallach, "A hazardous situation on the playground is one in which the user cannot see or evaluate the accident-causing problem. The potential for injury is thus hidden. Risk, on the other hand, allows the user to identify the challenge, evaluate the level of challenge and determine how to deal with it. Whether or not to cross a suspension bridge is a determination of risk, a bridge that falls because a rusted connector snapped when the child crossed the bridge is a hazard" (as cited in Jambor 1995, 7). Most playground injuries are caused by hazards rather than poor judgment in risk-taking (Jambor 1995).

Researchers are investigating the best strategies for providing children with outdoor risky play opportunities that minimize hazards, such as adventure playgrounds or the provision of unstructured play materials (loose parts) that can be freely manipulated in conventional playgrounds (Brussoni, Olsen, Pike, and Sleet 2012). Adventure playgrounds are filled with open-ended materials. They are based on the principle that children have control of their physical environment and can change it and add to it. Morgan Leichter-Saxby and Jill Wood compared injuries on a fixed-equipment playground with an adventure playground. Their research found that a statistically significant majority of play yard injuries occurred on the fixed-equipment playground. The adventure playground at the same school was found to be statistically safer. Their conclusion was that adventure playgrounds are safer because children can better control the risks. (2018). Eliminate real safety hazards and allow children to take risks.

Moving Forward

Now that you know the what, how, and why of transforming outdoor environments, it is time to take an in-depth look at enhancing individual play zones. As you move forward with your environment transformation, I hope that you will be encouraged by the ideas, stories, and visual images revealed in the following pages to create meaningful spaces for children to flourish.

Chapter 2
Art Studios

Teacher Brittany and the children have been talking about their own and others' unique facial features. She has listened intently to the children's understandings and misunderstandings about their similarities and differences. To further uncover their ideas, she decides to set up a provocation of loose parts for the children to create faces in the outdoor art studio. Before the children's arrival, Brittany gathers an eclectic selection, including bottle caps, spoons, metal rings and chain, glass stones, seashells, napkin rings, corks, yarn, and clothespins. She displays the loose parts in the middle of the table and arranges picture frames around the perimeter. Brittany observes children's ideas about identity as they represent their understanding through their representations and conversations. Sammy, age seven,

selects miniature artificial fir trees for his "hairy eyebrows." His eye design is symmetrical, complex, and layered. In the center of each eye is a large glass stone nested inside a metal napkin ring, resting on a metal decorating stencil disk. The design resembles the pupil inside the iris with the surrounding sclera, the white part of the eye, in the eye socket. Curiously, Sammy made his left eye blue and his right eye green. When prompted about the color choice, Sammy replied, "I like blue and green."

The Value of Art Studios

An outdoor art studio is a functional, visually appealing, and inspirational space for children. It is designed for art experiences such as drawing or painting with different media on surfaces and designing, modeling, or transforming materials in new ways. Doing art outdoors brings a whole new dimension to the creative process. The fresh air, fragrant smells, and sounds of nature stimulate the senses and nurture creativity. There is more freedom and less concern about mess. Children who may not venture into the indoor art area may be intrigued by outdoor art explorations.

Setting up an art studio as a sustainable art space is a wonderful way to reuse existing materials, reduce waste, and lower the amount spent on consumable goods while fostering creativity. Many loose parts are recycled materials or items from nature. Damion carefully places multicolored bottle caps inside a large picture frame positioned on the ground. His design fans out in lines. Practicing and modeling sustainability principles to young children can help them learn to value the environment. It lays the foundation for children to become environmentally responsible adults. Lakshmi creates a sculpture by inserting wire into holes of 2-by-8-inch corrugated plastic strips and connecting pieces. The honeycomb plastic sheets were discovered at a recycle store.

Know that children may want to keep their work if they have not used sustainable materials before or if taking art home is part of the current school culture. Taking a photograph to capture creations can be helpful and become documentation in a child's portfolio. Another option is "work in progress" signs that children can place on their work if they want to return to it. The more children use sustainable materials, the less likely they are to want to keep their work. The process, rather than the product, is what is important.

Schema Learning

Transporting: carrying materials to a work surface

Transforming: painting; mixing paints; creating pieces of art from loose parts; face painting; washing paint tools

Enclosing/enveloping: drawing enclosed spaces or shapes; working inside a picture frame; covering entire sheet of paper or canvas with paint; layering collage materials; covering hands in paint

Connecting/disconnecting: connecting pieces to make a representation; taking apart design pieces

Outdoor Art Studios to Foster Learning

1. Enhancing Social and Emotional Competencies

Having freedom to use art materials as desired builds self-confidence as children experience the results of their own choices, actions, and accomplishments. When children repeatedly use the same materials over time, they gain a sense of security and competence. For instance, leadership skills develop as Charlie shows her younger sister Bernadette how to brush water on slate before drawing, resulting in deeper and richer colors than marks left with dry chalk.

Children can express thoughts and feelings through art that may be overwhelming or seem unmanageable. Joey's family had to evacuate their home because of a flood. For a week, he has reenacted the evacuation and the damage to his home repeatedly with loose parts found in the art studio. The play gives him the assurance and understanding he seeks.

Children take turns and share materials and space. Mariano, Ari, and Alexa work at a table sharing a rotating container filled with natural loose parts. The container freely spins so that items are within reach as children express their needs to each other. Children also create pieces of art collaboratively.

2. Enhancing Language and Communication Competencies

Art is both a language and a process. Children's feelings, thoughts, ideas, and reactions are communicated through doing art. Art exploration opportunities help children symbolize their experiences. Children's language skills develop as they discuss materials, needs, explorations, and actions. Additionally, children are egocentric or self-absorbed and like to talk about their own creations. Working with loose parts without a prescribed outcome is relaxing and therapeutic. Spontaneous conversations occur and relationships develop as children casually talk to each other while doing art.

3. Enhancing Cognitive Competencies

When children engage with open-ended materials in an art studio, they explore and experiment, make decisions, solve problems, and develop concepts. Providing loose parts from the environment helps children interact more directly with their physical world and gain conceptual understandings. For example, a child's understanding of gravity is enhanced as a sculpture of tree blocks tumbles down. As children transform familiar objects into facial features, they expand their awareness of balance and symmetry and practice transferring visual information and memories onto a surface. Monica's knowledge of directionality increases as she creates a path in her design with tiles.

Math concepts of quantity, shape, size, weight, spatial relationships, and volume develop while working with art materials. While making representations, children discover that acorns, stones, pine cones, and seashells vary in shape, size, length, weight, and thickness. Children experience many geometric shapes in loose parts. For example, Leila combines several sticks to create a house, demonstrating how parts make a whole. Children identify, compare, and classify according to properties such as leather, metal, wood, glass, rubber, and plastic. They become aware of spatial limitations and organization as they place items such as metal rings on their work space.

4. Enhancing Physical Competencies

Physically handling art materials and tools strengthens and refines children's large and small motor skills. Muscular coordination of fingers, hands, and arms improves as children cradle, grasp, lift, place, reach, release, and scoop loose parts. Eye-hand coordination and visual-motor perception improves as a child reaches for items and places them on a work surface for exploring, making designs and patterns, or creating representations. Take Harper, who repeatedly makes sun designs with different loose parts. Today she selects cinnamon sticks and small green limpet seashells for her design. She cradles the shells in her right hand and uses the index finger and thumb of her left hand in a pincer grasp to pick up shells one at a time. "These shells are really tiny. I have to hold them tight." Children's hand and arm muscles increase through grasping and controlling tools and by exerting varying levels of pressure. Hand grips adjust depending on the shape and size of the tool or materials. Children grow to understand that a brush works best staying on the surface, but a potato masher works better going up and down. A thick piece of bark requires a different grip than a sea sponge. Using loose parts to create art also provides children with important sensory experiences. Children learn to recognize qualities and distinguish between them. For example, tree cookies come in a wide variety of colors, textures, smells, and weights.

5. Enhancing Expressive Arts

Open-ended art fosters curiosity, flexibility, innovation, investigation, and resourcefulness. Art in an outdoor studio with loose parts enhances children's creative expression, originality, and individuality. There is not a right or wrong way to create. For example, using her creativity and problem-solving skills, Avril selects loose parts that remind her of a turtle's body parts. There is a canning lid body, keys for legs, a rectangular metal ring for the tail, and a metal snap hook for the head. Last, she places small metal washers on top of the canning lid to represent the design on the turtle's back. When an art studio is filled with loose parts, children are in control of changing their ideas as they desire. The metal pieces Avril selects have been used by other children to create castles, robots, suns, insects, helicopters, monsters, people, and more. Because of the open-ended nature of loose parts, creative possibilities are infinite.

Essential Components: What Every Art Studio Needs

Space: Outdoor art studios work well on a patio, porch, or deck, especially with a cover that protects children on hot and rainy days so they may use the space almost all year long. Covers may include a pergola, gazebo, canopy, sunshade, or awning, which can be constructed or purchased at a big-box retail store. Umbrellas may be adjusted or moved as needed to shield against sun and rain. Art studios need to be inviting and beautiful. One way to enhance beauty is to surround the space with natural elements. Nestle the space next to trees, tall grasses, or bushes that provide variations in color and textures, or place plants in attractive ceramic pots nearby.

Work space: When designing an art studio, start with functionality. Materials need to be available and easily accessible, and there must be different spaces for creating. A hard work surface such as a tabletop is essential. For a group of twenty-four children, table space for six children is plenty, since not all children will be doing art at the same time. Consider setting up work space on the ground for children who like to spread out or are unable to sit at a table. This could be a low wooden platform or smooth carpeted area. Low benches, inverted crates, or tree trunks make unexpected work spaces. Display intriguing loose parts on the work top to invite exploration.

Create defined work areas with picture frames, large tiles, place mats, wood cutting boards, wood trays, and acrylic mirrors. These objects provide a visually appealing look in addition to defining space. Strive for a minimum surface size of 12 by 12 inches to accommodate children's creations. Place surfaces around the tabletop's perimeter, one frame in front of each chair. Note that children may create their own boundaries and place materials on top of, around, or inside designated work spaces.

For painting, an easel is a valuable investment. Standing at an easel to paint or draw provides whole-arm and total body movement. It is a different physical experience than painting or drawing while seated. A vertical mounted easel takes less space and can accommodate more children if made large. Easels can be handmade by a skilled volunteer and attached to a fence or building. Mount the easel so the easel paper is in front of the child's chest; for toddler and preschool children, the bottom of the easel is usually 18 to 24 inches off the ground. A generous size of 3 by 6 feet allows three to four children to paint alongside each other. Mount a paint tray at the easel's bottom to hold paint cups and catch drips, or set a small table nearby to hold paint containers. Include clips for children to put up and take down their own paintings, and stretch a clothesline with clothespins near the easel for drying.

This space was originally a secured play area for infants and toddlers in a family child care home. Green artificial turf covered the ground along with nylon tunnels, large pillows, a comforter, and plastic toys and furniture.

Art studio before

Art studio after

Once we decided to convert this space into an art studio, the turf was the first element to go. An outdoor parquet flooring installed on either side of the area gives warmth and is easy to hose off. A wide gravel strip with stepping-stones now welcomes children into the creative zone and divides the space in two. Mounted on the back fence is a 4- by 6-foot wooden easel. The wide easel allows several children to paint alongside each other. Wooden pallets are upcycled into a work surface by securing a thick sheet of acrylic to the top. Wood plates positioned on reed chargers define individual spaces for design work. A plant as a table centerpiece adds to the aesthetics. Tree trunks have been carved into chairs. Mark-making and design materials are stored in the portable metal caddy to be easily accessible.

Top Tips for Designing Art Studios

1. Group like items together.
2. Store materials in consistent containers.
3. Use sustainable materials for design and representational work.
4. Organize materials in a lazy Susan for easy access.
5. Designate work spaces by using place mats.
6. Make materials accessible to all children.
7. Fill the studio full of rich natural and manufactured materials that appeal to the senses and convey that this is an artist's area.

Enhancing art studios: A sustainable art studio is full of rich natural and manufactured materials that please your senses. Carefully select loose parts that are appealing to your visual sense (items of various forms, color, and size, such as discolored wood); tactile sense (pokey sycamore balls, smooth bark); olfactory sense (rosemary, pine cones); baric sense (pieces of heavy tree branches, stones); and auditory sense (metal rings, pieces of chain). Additional elements such as wind chimes, mobiles, metal wall décor, bamboo wall paneling, pottery, sculptures, and plants can provide inspiration and beauty.

Art Tools and Materials

Natural Loose Parts
Acorns
Bamboo
Bark
Catalpa pods
Cinnamon sticks
Corn husks
Driftwood
Eucalyptus pods
Flowers (dried)
Leaves
Oak galls
Palm tree bark
Pine cones
Pine needles
Rocks
Sea beans
Sea glass
Seashells
Seedpods
Sticks
Stones
Sycamore balls
Tree cookies
Twigs

Textiles
Burlap
Carpet samples
Fabric squares
Raffia
Ribbon
Shoelaces
String
Twine
Yarn

Tiles
Ceramic
Colored
Glass
Mosaic
Pebbles
Pool
Porcelain
River
Rock
Slate
Stone
Subway
Wall

Metal
Embroidery hoops
Film reels
Keys
Lids
Metal caps
Napkin rings
Nuts and bolts
Rings
Washers

Wood
Beads
Clothespins
Corks
Craft sticks
Embroidery hoops
Floor samples
Napkin rings
Picture frame samples
Scrap wood
Thread spools

Plastic*
Beads
Bottle caps
CD cases
Coffee stirrers
Corrugated sheets
Cups
Cylinders
Film canisters
Film spools
Marker caps
Napkin rings
Pipe
Pipe fittings
Tape spools
Tubes
Zip ties

Items to Designate Work Spaces
Acrylic mirrors (12 by 12 inches)
Picture frames
Place mats
Plates
Tiles (12 by 12 inches)
Trays
Wooden cutting boards

Art Materials
Bingo daubers
Cans or bowls for paint
Cans/containers for chalk, brushes, water
Canvas for each child
Chalk

Cleaning cloths	Paint	Water tubs for rinsing
Crates (to hold	Paintbrushes	brushes
canvases)	Pastels	Watercolor pencils
Crayons	Stand for paint cans	Watercolors
Markers	(tree trunk, crate,	Wire
	small table)	

* Select plastic items carefully and use recyclable objects from around your home. Consider materials that come in beautiful solid colors, such as bottle or marker caps. Avoid plastics such as yogurt containers that are covered in printed pictures and words that do not add to design aesthetics.

Place mats define the work space.

Working on
the ground offers
new creative
perspectives.

Storage and Organization

Materials for an outdoor studio are intended to stay outside to save time and energy bringing materials in and out. Convenient storage and organization are necessary. Heavy-duty shelves or secure and stable bench tops can display materials. Three- or four-tier shelf organizers provide storage space. Purchase shelving or construct it by securing thick, wide planks of solid wood on concrete blocks or tree trunks.

Organize items in shallow containers and on shelving units to keep the work space ordered, clutter-free, and clean. This helps children find items easily and make selections independently. Consider containers such as metal baskets that can stand up to outdoor weather. Wicker baskets will hold up for a season or two if kept under cover. Containers with sections are particularly good for displaying materials.

Arrange loose parts by categories such as color, material, or shape. For instance, place all items together that are blue or metal, or make a collection of items that are all round. Display materials in a container that has a similar property: circular materials in a round container or metal items in a metal one. Set up an invitation to explore familiar items by attractively

Containers with compartments work well for storing materials.

placing materials on a tabletop. A wooden bowl or basket with compartments enhances natural materials such as pine cones, tree cookies, seashells, and sea glass.

Standard mark-making materials extend exploration possibilities. These materials can be stored in cans, bamboo boxes, or containers with sections. If children ask for glue, explain that sustainable artwork is temporary and lasts for a short time. It is all about placing materials in a thoughtful way. If a child asks to take an art creation home, talk about being able to reuse the beautiful materials, and take a photo of their work.

In a sustainable art space most explorations are done with loose parts, so water access isn't usually needed for cleanup unless children are painting.

Mark-making tools are stored together.

Paint supplies are available for children to access on their own.

Cleaning and Maintaining the Space

Predictability is important for children, so keep art materials organized and in consistent spaces in the studio. Too many material options can be overwhelming, so be selective. Children can be guided to return materials and clean up when they are finished. Loose parts need to be sorted and returned to designated containers. Children are especially good at helping with classification. Rotate or add new items when children's interest seems to be waning. For example, change out plastic bottle caps for tiles or add cinnamon sticks to natural materials. Sometimes new elements spark renewed interest. Check daily for broken pieces and safety hazards. Consumable materials such as markers or chalk need to be replenished when depleted. At the easel, children can independently get paint and clean up when finished. Provide a tub of water nearby for children to place their used brushes and containers. These materials will need to be washed daily. Paint on an art easel can stay. A paint-covered easel adds to the studio's aesthetics. Other daily tasks include disinfecting tabletops and blowing or sweeping floor surfaces.

The Extra Dimension

Consider using canvas rather than paper as an authentic and sustainable painting surface that children will paint over repeatedly. Artists paint on canvas, and children love to use materials of real artists. Throughout history it has been common practice for artists to paint over their work, particularly when canvas was scarce. Remember that children enjoy the process of painting rather than the final product. Provide a canvas (16 by 20 inches) for each child with their name written on the back. Keep canvases accessible by storing them in a crate or leaning them against a wall or fence. When children want to paint, they get their canvas and place it on the easel. Set up a paint station so children may mix their own paint colors. Include small metal bowls, brushes, paint, a tub of water, and rags. Small pet bowls work well, as they are designed not to tip. Have pint-sized bottles of paint (16 ounces) for children to squeeze out desired amounts on their palette (bowl). Children can place their palette on a small worktable next to the easel and begin painting. When finished, children

clean brushes and bowls in a washtub and set their canvas aside to dry. Children continue to paint on their canvas throughout the year. The paint will become thick, dry, and crackly as more layers are added, creating amazing textures. When the paint is very thick, the canvas can be sent home and a new one started.

Supporting Equitable Learning

- Allow plenty of time for children to experiment with art materials.
- Create access and space to engage in art explorations for children who are nonmobile, use walkers or wheelchairs, or need adaptive seating. Set up art experiences on the floor, on a wall, or under a table.
- Include materials that allow for expansive work, such as very large paper or large slabs of slate.
- Encourage divergent thinking and unconventional solutions to problems, and allow children to use materials in different ways.
- Offer tools of different shapes, sizes, and textures to accommodate varying grasps so children may successfully use tools and materials.
- Encourage children to collaborate with others on group art explorations, such as creating a collage mural with found materials.
- Communicate with children about how they are using tools, and encourage children to describe their actions, feelings, and thoughts.

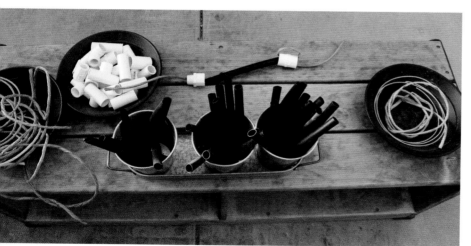

Area rugs next to an open storage shelf provide a comfortable surface to engage with materials.

An old greenhouse was converted into an outdoor art studio.

Infant/Toddler Art Studio Ideas

Infants and toddlers depend on us to offer art experiences and foster creative explorations. Create a safe space in an art studio to nurture their curiosity. Mark making and painting are fascinating to infants and toddlers.

Mark-making experiences: Surfaces for drawing need to be low or on the ground for infants and toddlers. A large slate tile provides a durable drawing surface and is reusable and easy to clean. Offer large pieces of chalk for infants or toddlers to make marks. When finished, wipe the slate with a damp cloth.

Painting experiences: Art canvases or big pieces of cardboard provide wonderful painting surfaces for infants and toddlers, as they are durable and can hold lots of paint. Set a canvas or cardboard on the ground or provide a tabletop easel that can sit firmly on the floor. Toddlers can be independent in selecting their own brushes and paint color but will need help getting paint. Toddlers can place used paintbrushes into a pan of soapy water.

Chapter 3
Clay Studios

As Diana (age three) joins Alexa (age four) and me at the clay table, she shares how she had played cats with her mom and dad all weekend. According to teacher Cheri, Diana loves cats and often dresses in cat attire that includes a cat tail, collar, and headband with cat ears. I glance over and notice that Diana is wearing a shirt with an image of a cat's face on it. Hearing about her love for cats inspires me to tell the girls about my trip to the small medieval village of La Romieu in southwest France last spring and the legend of Angeline and the cats. I show the girls photographs on my cell phone of the cat statues hidden around La Romieu and ask if they can find them. The girls are excited to find the statue in each photo of a cat peering out of a window, walking across an awning, or ready to pounce from a high ledge. They give an enthusiastic "yes" when I ask if they want to make a cat statue for Angeline. I watch intently as Diana begins to mold the soft, pliable clay. She carefully shapes a large oval lump of clay into the body and then attaches another large ball for the cat's head. Ears are formed as she pinches pointed triangles at the top of the ball. Diana giggles as she tilts the cat's head a bit to the side. "I think that it is a curious cat." The tilted head does indeed give the cat a quizzical look. I wonder if this adjustment is accidental or intentional. Diana rolls a piece of clay back and forth between her palm and the table to make a long, thick tail. She attaches it to the cat's backside and adjusts it several times until she finally appears satisfied with the way it angles up and then down toward the cat's back. Alexa too shapes and molds her cat with an oblong body and circular-shaped head. The back of her cat slants downward as the hind legs are half the length of the front ones. The next day Bernadette (age two) and Charlie (age five) join the cat sculpting. Bernadette rolls and presses clay balls on the cat form for legs that stick straight out from the body. Charlie's cat has a flat face. She picks up a modeling tool to create fine details and markings. "My cat has fur like this." She uses the tool to add texture by drawing tiny lines in the moist surface. "Ta-da! Almost finished. She just needs whiskers." Many renderings of cat sculptures appear over the next week as each artist provides their own interpretations.

The Value of Clay Studios

Few art materials are as captivating, enjoyable, and full of creative potential as natural clay. A clay studio is a space for children to express their energy, creativity, emotions, and ideas. Sculpting with clay is a unique, creative, sensory experience for children of all ages. Infants and toddlers delight in exploring the physical aspects of clay through pounding, patting, smelling, poking, grasping, and mouthing, while older children may sculpt familiar places, people, and things. Unlike play dough, clay is a sustainable, natural material from the earth that has an unlimited shelf life when stored properly. Clay work is not saved but recovered for the next day's explorations, instilling the essential values of reusing and recycling. If you have not experienced clay, I encourage you to try it so that you know firsthand what it is like to manipulate this soft, pliable substance. If children have not been offered many occasions to use clay, they will need time to become familiar with it and its malleability. It is essential to have clay available regularly so that children learn how to master clay skills and techniques over time.

Schema Learning

Transforming: molding clay into infinite shapes

Enclosing/enveloping: making rolled pieces into circles or enclosed organic shapes; covering your hand in clay; wrapping

Rotating: rolling clay

Connecting/disconnecting: putting pieces of clay together; tearing or breaking clay into pieces; smashing clay

Clay Studios to Foster Learning

1. Enhancing Social and Emotional Competencies

Clay is malleable, pliable, and responsive to children's needs and emotions. Working with clay is therapeutic and a powerful way to release feelings and energy. Tensions relax and anxieties decrease as children mold and manipulate the tactile medium. For instance, five-year-old Xochitl returns to her child care after being at home for several weeks during the COVID-19 pandemic. During the pandemic, her daily routine was disrupted and she was cared for by different adults. She worried about getting sick with the virus and about her grandfather getting sick. Her family experienced economic difficulties. Working with clay allows her to process her feelings and try to make sense of the past weeks. Clay is forgiving and can be remolded and envisioned, unlike a permanent crayon mark or paint stroke. Children feel powerful and in control as they punch a ball of clay until it becomes flat. It is as if they are conveying, "I am in charge and have influence." Children understand, "I can repair mistakes and not be afraid to make them." If children are unsatisfied with their work, they simply squish it and begin again. Competency, independence, initiative, and satisfaction develop as a child creates unique shapes.

At Roong Aroon School in Thailand, I observe as two boys, Kusa and Phet, dig fistfuls of clay from the large clay storage pot and place it in their pail. They grasp the pail's handle together and transport the heavy load to their clay boards. They kneel next to their boards, pull out clay, and begin to knead it. Kusa shares how he uses his thumbs to soften the clay. Phet comments that he prefers to use the force from his shoulders and press down with his palms. Kusa tries out Phet's technique and discovers that he likes it better than his own way. As they manipulate the clay, the boys share experiences about playing football (soccer). These boys are becoming increasingly socially competent and cooperative in their interactions with peers. While working with clay, they pay attention to each other's work and ideas, communicate confidently, and see things from another's point of view. Another way to present clay to promote social engagement is to place it as one large block on a table for a group of children to work on together, learning to compromise, collaborate, and share tools, space, and ideas.

2. Enhancing Language and Communication Competencies

A magical thing happens as children experience clay's workability. They automatically begin to talk freely to others around the table about their ideas and what they are doing. Vocabulary builds as children learn new words to describe their efforts, such as *pound, pinch, roll, flatten, poke, tear, squeeze, coil, stretch, squash, twist,* and *bend.* Educators can extend children's vocabulary by using rich language to describe children's technical actions, such as *sculpting, etching, coiling,* and *modeling.*

Working with clay develops different language functions of a child's speech, as proposed by M. A. K. Halliday (2004):

Instrumental: Language that fulfills a need: "I need more clay."

Regulatory: Language that influences others' behavior: "Hey, you need to pound it flat like this."

Interactional: Language that builds and maintains social relationships: "How did you get the clay out (of the cylinder)?"

Personal: Language that expresses personal feelings, preferences, and identity: "I like to roll the clay to make a worm."

Heuristic: Language used to explore, discover, and learn: "Why are the pieces not sticking?"

Imaginative: Language used to explore the imagination: "Let's pretend that this is a volcano island."

Informative or representational: Language that conveys facts and information: "We'll add dinosaurs near the volcano because they ruled the earth."

3. Enhancing Cognitive Competencies

The changeability, adaptability, and pliability of clay presents limitless problem-solving opportunities for children. When Joshua has a preconceived object in mind, such as a bowl, he must figure out how to hollow out the solid clay ball and make a bottom and sides. He may begin to press and pull the clay or push his thumb into the middle and then pinch up the walls. He may encounter challenges in creating walls of even thickness or in fixing collapsing walls. Another day he may squeeze the clay into a long snake or roll it back and forth on a smooth, flat surface to create a coil, experimenting with applying even pressure. How does the clay's stiffness or softness alter his approach? Children construct knowledge through active exploration and manipulation of clay. Each new experience presents opportunity to build cause-and-effect, problem-solving, and critical-thinking competency. As children explore clay, they notice, wonder, and question. "How do I get rid of an air bubble?" "What happens if clay gets too wet?" Then they investigate to find out answers to their questions. Explorations may lead to new questions and inquiries, such as discovering that the clay's surface can be textured using tools or found objects.

Children grasp spatial relationships as they recognize different views of a clay sculpture. An ability to compare, match, and sort objects develops as a child organizes and classifies balls of clay in order of size: Aaron measures length as he rolls clay into long and short worms. Isabella considers weight as she states, "Heavy! It's too heavy!" Children study volume while shaping clay into cubes, cones, cylinders, spheres, and irregular forms. Veronica builds an understanding of conservation, knowing that she has the same amount of clay even if she rolls it into a long snake or breaks it up into multiple pieces. Saul increases his knowledge of qualitative change, stating that his clay tower is higher than Samuel's. Tara demonstrates comprehension of addition as she adds a piece to her clay, subtraction as she removes a piece, and division as she separates her clay into pieces.

4. Enhancing Physical Competencies

Clay softens by warming and kneading it in your hands. Manipulating a piece of clay helps develop a child's large and small muscles, improving dexterity. Clay requires more hand strength than play dough. As children handle clay, they use a variety of motor actions, including squishing, squeezing, pulling, pushing, pinching, flattening, digging, and shredding. As Diana presses clay into a tin can, she comments, "I'm using my muscles to put it in tight." Eye-hand coordination increases as eyes and hands work together. More complex hand and finger skills develop as children transition from using hands to clay tools for shaping, smoothing, refining, and finishing work. There are sensory benefits to working with clay: visual sense (light, gray, buff, red), tactile sense (wet, dry, slippery), olfactory sense (earthy, damp); baric sense (heavy, heavier, lighter), thermic sense (cool, warm), and auditory sense (squishy, smacking).

5. Enhancing Expressive Arts

Sculpting is another way for children to express ideas and understandings about their world. Exploring this pliable medium presents unanticipated discoveries. Clay forms can represent recalled objects or experiences. Working with a three-dimensional medium releases new possibilities for creativity, imagination, and self-expression. Clay work offers an opportunity to learn unfamiliar techniques, tools, and vocabulary. With ample time to explore, children may discover how to pinch and roll clay on their own or by observing others. Teachers can expand learning by showing various hand-building methods: pinch (squeezing clay between thumb and finger), coil (attaching rolls of clay together to form walls), and slab (shaping clay into a broad, flat, thick piece). The joining techniques of scoring and slip help clay pieces stick together. Scoring involves scratching clay pieces before attaching them together. Slip is a mixture of clay and water used to join scored pieces of clay. These techniques make it possible for children to better represent their ideas in clay. As children work with clay, teachers can talk about art elements: line, shape, color, value, form, space, and texture. Point out how a sculpture has height, width, and depth and can be viewed from multiple angles (form). Comment on how the surface of a piece has a rough, gritty look (texture) or how the rolled pieces look thick and strong (line).

During children's first encounters with clay, they use all their senses and motor skills to discover its fascinating properties. They press their fingers into it, poke it, and examine it by banging, patting, squishing, smelling, scraping, and dropping it. Controlled exploration follows as children make basic shapes, flattening the clay into pieces and rolling it in the shape of rope or a ball. Children next begin to name their clay forms. For example, Edwin states that stacked clay balls are a snowman. Finally, children plan first, decide what to make, and then create the form. This is seen as Martin creates a nest with eggs and worms for the chicks to eat after they hatch. During each modeling stage, children express countless original ideas and characterize them. Children's divergent thinking, intrinsic motivation, and persistence show in their creativity and curiosity. Creating with clay brings true delight and satisfaction.

Essential Components: What Every Clay Studio Needs

Space: A clay studio can be integrated into the art studio or designed in its own private space. Select a shady space, as heat will dry out clay. The space can be as small as a tabletop. The floor should be concrete or a wipeable surface.

Work space: Every potter needs a sturdy worktable and space to store tools. Stability and durability are important as children will be exerting force as they pound and manipulate clay. Commercial ceramic worktables are not an option as they are designed for adults and are not modifiable. Drawings and designs for pottery worktables on the internet can be shortened to accommodate young children. The best option is a well-made child-sized table. Table shape does not really matter if two to six children can work at the same time. There needs to be room for clay or wedging boards (12 by 12 inches) at each work space. Some children will prefer to work standing up. Clay is worked on clay boards; however, clay work often spills over on to the tabletop and ground. If desired, oilcloth, canvas, or thick plastic can be used to cover the table, all available by the yard at fabric and hardware stores. If using oilcloth, select a neutral, solid color rather than a floral print.

Play dough and plastic cookie cutters were the standard sensory material and tools for many years at this center. After discussing the many benefits of clay, the teacher was challenged to consider replacing the play dough.

Natural tools including sticks, stones, shells, acorns, and wood slices are attractively displayed on wooden crates that serve as a low, accessible shelving unit. A sturdy wrought iron coffee table is upcycled for a worktable, and 12-by-12-inch plywood squares provide a defined work space. The clay is covered with a damp fabric to keep it moist.

Enhancing clay studios: Little stifles creativity more than a bare environment. Inject interest into the studio by displaying pottery and adding plants, herbs, tree branches, or flowers in appealing pots. Increase visual appeal by including decorative ceramic tiles or artfully clustering sculptures together. Tools can be arranged in a clay pitcher or beautiful wicker basket. Create a rustic design by adding weathered materials, repurposed objects, organic shapes, natural textures, and earthy tones.

Top Tips for Designing Clay Studios

1. Use a sturdy and durable worktable.
2. Store real or natural tools and accessories in rustic containers.
3. Keep clay moist so it remains soft and pliable.
4. Provide an ideal working surface by covering boards with canvas cloth.
5. If possible, locate studio in a place with a concrete floor that can be hosed down.
6. Display ceramic pieces for inspiration.

Clay Tools and Materials

Clay: Clay comes in different types and colors. Porcelain clay is the best clay for using with children. It is an all-purpose clay that is suitable for exploration and sculpting. It is light gray in color, smooth, soft, and responsive. This clay is available at art stores and ceramic companies. I discovered that porcelain clay is used in college ceramic classes, and I have purchased it at a local college bookstore.

Work space surfaces: Clay boards (12-by-12-inch canvas-covered plywood) are a portable work surface that may be purchased or handmade. Boards that are specifically designed for clay are worth the investment, as they are durable, will not stick to clay, dry quickly, and will last a long time. These boards prevent the frustration of scouring off sticky pieces and can be scraped and sponged down for easy cleanup. Canvas can be purchased by the yard, stretched over a piece of 12-by-12-inch plywood, and stapled on the backside. Have water or wet paper towels available for children to moisten their hands as needed.

Setup Materials

Clay boards or wooden cutting boards

Clay cutter (wire clay cutter, dental floss, string)

Small bucket or tub of water (for children to moisten their sponges or paper towels)

Water holders (sponges, paper towels, small bowls, plastic spray bottle)

Clay Tools

Boxwood tools such as ribs and scrapers (modeling tools for creating fine details and markings)

Forks and spoons

Mallets

Ribbon and wire loop tools

Rolling pins

Wooden dowels

Accessory Materials

Acorns

Combs

Craft sticks/sticks

Eucalyptus pods

Large wooden beads

Nuts, bolts, washers

Old toothbrushes

Seashells

Stones

Wire

Cleanup Materials

Buckets for cleanup water

Cloth towels

Scrapers

The smooth mahogany bark of manzanita pieces are beautiful and durable clay tools.

Storage and Organization

Tools, accessories, and clay boards may be stored on shelves in shallow crates, baskets, or containers. Arrange crates to create a storage unit that is functional and rustic in design. An open utility shelf under a table is another option. To keep clay moist and workable for long periods of time, it needs to be stored in an airtight container such as heavy-duty plastic bags and plastic buckets or containers with airtight lids. I prefer storing clay in plastic bags with damp cloths, placing the bags in a beautiful wide-mouth ceramic pot. To store clay, roll clay into softball-sized balls when children are finished. Poke your thumb into the ball to create a hollow cylinder. Pour water into the hole and squeeze the clay together to cover the opening. Wrap clay balls in damp cloths and place into a sealed container. This will keep the clay moist until the next use. Do not fret if stored clay becomes rock hard. Rehydrate it by placing it in a sealable bag, sprinkling in some water, letting out the air, sealing the bag, and dropping it into a bucket of water for 15 minutes.

Cleaning and Maintaining the Space

Do not allow clay to go down the drain. Always have children rinse their hands in a bucket of water and pour the water in a safe location outside. The slurry clay at the bottom of the bucket can be used later.

Health and safety: Clay dust from dry clay presents a potential health concern, so it is essential to wipe accumulating clay dust from clay boards and tabletops with a damp sponge or cloth at cleanup time. Do not use a brush or broom. It is helpful to have two sponges: one for removing clay and a second for wiping off residue. A scraper can remove excess wet clay before sponging. Hose down or use a damp mop on the floor as needed.

The Extra Dimension

Clay head sculptures present a unique experience. To make a head sculpture, start with a Styrofoam wig head (for short hair) and a nontopple base that has a dowel. Press the Styrofoam wig head onto the dowel and smoothly cover the entire head with a thick 1-inch layer of clay. Children can then add or sculpt varying types of facial features and hair. Sculptures may be saved and reused. Wipe excess clay from the base and add it back to the clay form. Smooth out clay over forms. Cover the head with moist cotton towels, and then cover the entire base and head with a plastic garbage bag. Secure the bag.

Supporting Equitable Learning

- Clay is gluten-free and safe for children who have a gluten allergy.
- Place a tarp on the floor and set a block of clay in the center. This allows nonmobile children to have access to the clay.
- Offer tools for children who may not want to use their fingers to shape clay.
- Provide tools of different shapes and sizes to accommodate various grasps.
- Bring in pottery from various places and cultures to increase children's understanding of the differences and similarities between themselves and people from other backgrounds and countries. For example, bring in Chinese porcelains, Peruvian clay figures, Mexican earthenware, and Japanese teacups.

A low table is the perfect height for toddlers to investigate cool, damp clay.

Alexa and Diana make lollipops with balls of clay topped with seashells on sticks.

Infant/Toddler Clay Studio Ideas

Infants and toddlers enjoy exploring the physical aspects of clay with their hands. No tools are necessary and in fact can interfere with the sensory connection between hands and clay. A low platform surface on the ground is ideal for infants and toddlers to access clay. Clay can be set on a piece of plywood or canvas mat or placed in a large, shallow container. Consider presenting clay in a block the first few times to see how children respond. Allow children to become familiar with clay and its wonderful responsive properties before putting out tools. Once children's desire for tools is apparent, add tools for pounding, such as potato mashers and rubber mallets, and tools for digging and poking, such as sturdy sticks, round wooden clothespins, and cabinet door handles.

Chapter 4
Sound Gardens

The outdoor platform transforms into a venue for a live music performance. Alexa (age three) and Drew (age three), the musical ensemble, enter the stage with a rhythm stick in each hand. Before them are three overturned galvanized tubs of different sizes. Alexa is a charismatic drum player whose abundant joy radiates as she plays. She bends, twists, and wiggles as she simultaneously plays buckets on either side of her with both hands. Drew stands stiff and straight with his feet together. He beats a single bucket in a right, left, right, left pattern. Suddenly, Alexa's arms reach high above her head and she lunges in front of Drew to strike a tub with her right stick. She jumps back. Drew moves into Alexa's space, extends his left arm over her body, and taps the tub in front of her. Although smaller than Drew, Alexa does not relinquish her space but simply adjusts her movements. Her actions drive Drew back to his tub. Alexa's rhythm ability and agility are impressive, as are her spunk and capacity to hold her own. The two friends continue to strike tubs, their beats now in unison as the music reaches a crescendo.

The Value of Sound Gardens

Children are persistent and natural music makers. They explore music enthusiastically, relentlessly, and spontaneously. Young children are intrigued by sound-producing objects, particularly when they are the ones creating the sounds. A sound garden is designed for sound exploration, offering children a rich repertoire of materials. Surrounded by the beauty of nature and found materials, it fosters joy, exuberance, and engagement with unusual physical objects such as trash cans, pots, tubes, and containers for children to discover and strike with utensils in fascinating ways. Unlike a real instrument, there is no particularly correct way to make sound with loose parts. It does not require any expertise, aptitude, or age, so all children can create sounds that please them. It is exhilarating to bang, pound, and bash, and nobody wants to stop because it sounds and feels so good.

Sound Gardens to Foster Learning

1. Enhancing Social and Emotional Competencies

With the freedom to make sound, children can express feelings and release tension, such as when Misha uses a wooden spoon to forcefully strike inverted paint cans. Hitting in an appropriate way is a natural stress reducer for her. Playing music is emotionally balancing; it connects us to our deepest selves. Children practice self-control in a state of excitement, patience while waiting for a turn, and perseverance to improve their technique. If a sound or beat does not work out as desired, there is immediate opportunity for a child to adjust, repeat, or recover. Instant mastery promotes self-esteem, and confidence develops as children select and experiment with materials. Joy and laughter result as children begin to improvise with one another, feeling a sense of belonging. Social skills of sharing, contributing, leading, and following develop as children share space and materials, show consideration for and cooperation with others, and mutually help one another.

2. Enhancing Language and Communication Competencies

Music is like language. It has rhythm, dynamics, pitch, tempo, and expression. As infants we start by making sounds and soon imitate the speech patterns around us. Children must learn to distinguish speech sounds, sound combinations, and inflections to master language, and they must do the same with music. Experimenting with sound in a sound garden enhances a child's listening skills and sense of rhythm, which are essential to language development. Nate steadily strikes the muffin tin in a recurring pattern, illustrating an understanding of duplicating sound patterns. Language and music both include dynamics, or the overall volume level of sound. People speak loudly when they are angry or want to be heard and softly perhaps if they do not want to be noticed. Just as with language, sounds played loudly give a very different message than sounds played softly. Joseph varies the volume of his hits from loud, powerful crashes to quieter ringing sounds. Language and music both demonstrate tempo or speed. Our speech is fast to show excitement and slow to create suspense. As Lucas pounds on inverted trash cans, most of his taps are very rapid in succession, but occasionally he slows their speed to recharge his energy. Language and music both express emotions and ideas. Think about how a feeling such as happiness, surprise, anger, or sadness can be communicated with words and music.

3. Enhancing Cognitive Competencies

Making noise is important for children, although some adults find loud noise irritating. Fortunately, sound gardens are created outdoors. Remember that along with being loud and messy, young children are natural scientists. They try out, test, evaluate, and try again. Through this experimentation, they develop anticipation and prediction, make discoveries, and determine what works and what does not. A sound garden is a laboratory for exploring the science of sound. Will different types of striking utensils produce different sounds? How about smaller or larger spoons? Wooden or metal? Slotted or solid? What sounds can be created by a spatula, paint stirrer, rubber mallet, or wire whisk? How does sound change when Ashley hits a metal pie pan, bowl, or colander or a wire or solid serving tray? What kinds of sound can be created when she runs a wire whisk along a corrugated pipe or broiling rack? In the sound garden, children discover, listen, tinker, and think about expressive qualities of a variety of sounds.

4. Enhancing Physical Competencies

Exploring loose parts in a sound garden supports the development of children's physical abilities. Manual dexterity, object manipulation, and eye-hand coordination improve as children grasp a mallet or wooden spoon to beat pots and pans. Each striking utensil requires a different grip, resulting in strong, coordinated hand and arm muscles. Children practice body control such as balancing, stopping, and starting when they pound loaf pans anchored to a trellis. Angel food cake pans and hubcaps suspended from tree branches allow Spencer to explore temporal awareness, the internal understanding of the relationship between movement and time. Temporal awareness is essential in developing a sense of rhythm. This is seen as Spencer works on his timing by tapping the pans as they swing back and forth. Agility develops as Marisa and Evan march around the yard drumming on trash can lids. Playing trash cans as drums is a full-body workout requiring arm, core, and lower-body strength as children stand and move while playing. Drumming also helps children learn to control their movements.

While generating sounds, children explore actively with all their senses, including sight, sound, touch, and movement and body awareness. The process by which the brain organizes and interprets this sensory information is known as sensory integration. The assimilation of sensory information with motor activities is called motor planning. Through repeated practice of beating buckets with a spoon in each hand, Tenesha can now drum proficiently without thinking about it. Playing drums in the sound garden has improved her motor planning ability as well as her auditory focusing, attending, and concentration skills.

5. Enhancing Expressive Arts

Creative intelligence is the ability to go beyond what currently exists to create innovative ideas. Enhance creativity by providing children with many different opportunities. Intriguing loose parts in a sound garden that are suspended or displayed in unusual ways beckon curiosity. These sound-producing items can create an imaginary world. Children tend to be very creative, perhaps because of their innate curiosities. A child can discover multiple ways to use a spoon, while an adult thinks of it only for eating. Making music by banging pots and pans may transport you back to your own childhood. Perhaps you marched around your neighborhood as you struck a hubcap cymbal with a stick. Maybe you transformed a plank of wood into a guitar, made a cookie tin into a drum, or turned a tin can into a microphone. Making unique sounds with familiar objects in a sound garden with no objective in mind is enjoyable and creative.

Essential Components: What Every Sound Garden Needs

Space: The space should be located away from the classroom building and quieter areas to accommodate loud sounds. Grass or play yard bark work well as ground surfaces; though a textured surface that makes sound as you walk on it, such as crushed gravel, adds a sound element. Locating the play zone along the perimeter of the yard on a fence or in a corner are good options. Noise may be a challenge if the sound garden is near neighbors. A tree with low-hanging branches is perfect for suspending loose parts.

Work space: Sound gardens are exceptionally fun to create. It is simple and inexpensive to gather items and turn them into a whimsical garden for sound exploration. For starters, you need a sturdy structure from which items can be attached or suspended. This could be a fence, building side, trellis, plant stand, pallet, arbor, or tree. If a free-standing frame is selected, it needs to be secure to prevent tipping.

Take delight in discovering ordinary and unusual items such as galvanized pans and trays to fasten to the foundation and serve as instruments. Search your own home as well as garage sales, salvage yards, thrift stores, hardware stores, and educator resource centers. Be certain to walk up and down every store aisle and check every bin, as you never know what unexpected find might provide inspiration. Look for items of varying materials, size, shape, and design. Put on your tinkering lens and think about how an object might be upcycled to create sound. During one of my outings, I discovered 20- to 32-inch water heater drain pans. Children were drawn to the pans because of their bigness. Choose materials made from different substances—metal, rubber, wood, and so on—so children can compare sounds. Secure items with handles or holes with zip ties, wire, rope, string, fishing line, or electrical tie-downs. Know that screwing the top and bottom of an item may limit vibration and alter the sound produced.

Plan how to arrange objects before permanently fastening them. Clustering like items together in odd numbers generates visual interest. Hang objects low enough for children to reach. Encourage sound variations by including items to strike, such as buckets, pans, and trays; things to run a stick across, such as an oven rack, corrugated black pipe, or corrugated metal roof panel; and pieces that chime or ring, such as metal triangles or wind chimes. The neat thing about a sound garden is that you can start small and add new pieces anytime inspiration strikes.

Invert galvanized and plastic tubs and buckets in various sizes on the ground or a platform to make a drum station. Large tubs are available at hardware and feed stores as well as at tractor supply companies. Do not forget trash can lids, which children can bang with a striker as if they are cymbals.

Sound garden before

The space surrounding this beautiful tree is full of unrelated plastic play furniture—a sand table, kitchen, and mailbox. The designed purpose of the space is unclear.

Sound garden after

After removing the plastic play furniture, the ground surface was prepared with gravel and river rock for a natural look that complements the reed fencing. Black metal cabinet doors are upcycled as a base to secure metal trays. The black metal provides a visually appealing background to highlight the trays. Like items are clustered together: metal trays hang on the fence and stove-top burner covers are suspended from tree branches. Materials are various sizes and made from different substances so sounds can be compared. Striking utensils are kept in a container on the ground. Trees and plants add beauty and sensory appeal.

Enhancing sound gardens: Surround the landscape with varying textures, colors, and scents to engage the senses and add appeal to sound exploration. One of the simplest ways to add texture and color to a space is to bring in new shrubs or plants along with crunching gravel, boulders, tree trunks, or river rock to add dimension and interest. Herbs such as rosemary, sage, mint, or thyme provide a wonderful fragrance. Consider hanging wind chimes in breezy areas or planting several varieties of grasses to rustle against each other. Rattlesnake quaking grass has tiny blooms shaped like rattlesnake rattles that clatter in the breeze.

Top Tips for Designing Sound Gardens

1. Use upcycled items as strikers and items to strike.
2. Group metal trays and tubs together.
3. Provide corrugated and smooth metal items along with wooden and metal uten sils to offer comparison.
4. Keep striking utensils easily accessible.
5. Hang noise-producing objects from tree branches, fences, or walls within children's reach.
6. Take advantage of natural surroundings to provide visual and sensory interest.

Sound Garden Tools and Materials

Items to Strike	Gourds	*Striking Utensils (wood and metal)*
Angel food cake pan	Loaf pan	Bamboo pieces
Baking sheet	Metal tray	Dowel
Black corrugated drainage pipe	Muffin pan	Ladle
Bread pan	Nana bell	Masher
Broiler rack	Pie pan	Mesh strainer
Bucket	Pots and pans	Paint stirrer
Bundt pan	Roasting pan	Pasta server
Cake pan	Serving tray	Slotted spoon
Canning rings	Springform pan	Spatula
Cannoli form tubes	Tart rings	Splatter guard
Colander	Tin cans of various sizes	Spoon
Cookie sheet	Trash can (metal and rubber)	Stick
Cooling rack	Trash can lid	Stirring spoon
Corrugated metal roof panel	Wind chimes	Strainer
Fluted tube pan	Wooden bowls	Tongs
		Whisk

Metal trampoline pipes were upcycled into a hanging xylophone.

Large water heater drain pans are waiting to be played

Black iron cabinet doors serve as a striking background for metal trays.

Storage and Organization

Organize striking utensils in containers located at the base of the sound garden. Any type of metal container will do if it will not topple over: metal pots, planters, pitchers, caddies, canisters, baskets, toolboxes, milk cans, or compartment baskets. Consider suspending utensils from hooks attached to the fence. For example, hang a wire whisk on the fence next to metal trays.

Cleaning and Maintaining the Space

Materials in a sound garden need to be extremely durable to survive repeated banging. When possible, select items made from galvanized or stainless steel, which will hold up to exterior and coastal exposures over long periods of time. Plastic and rubber materials hold up as well. Metal surfaces that rust can be sealed with a protective paint, or objects can be replaced once rusted. At the end of each day, retrieve strikers that have found their way around the play yard. Be on the lookout for interesting items to add to the sound garden over time.

The Extra Dimension

A music rod made with a threaded metal rod and washers brings unexpected delight to a sound garden. Children slide the washers to the top of the threaded rod and then let them go. As the washers cascade down, they sound like rain falling. Instructions for making a music rod are available on several internet sites.

Supporting Equitable Learning

- Recognize that all children have musical potential.
- Display items at different levels and heights, including on the ground.
- Have a variety of loose parts available to play as instruments.
- Include an assortment of striking tools that require different grips.
- Incorporate cookie tins, wooden salad bowls, and tubs as drums, as advanced fine motor skills are not required to hit them.
- Consider alternatives to kitchen items. Some families may not wish for their children to use kitchen items as instruments for cultural reasons.
- Have children who do not hear sound put their hands on buckets and tubs to feel vibrations.
- Allow active and loud sound making.
- Create a safe sound garden for children with noise sensitivity that includes quieter options such as hand bells, bottles of sand, gourds, rubber trash cans, and bamboo xylophones.
- Use music to release energy.
- Encourage children of all ages and abilities to play.

Hubcaps suspended in barrel rings create different clanging sounds when hit with a utensil.

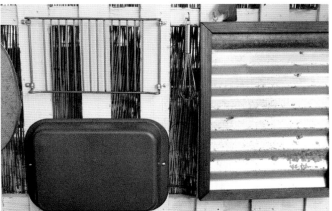

Toddlers enjoy making sounds on inverted trash cans.

Ridges of corrugated metal make an intriguing clattering sound.

Infant/Toddler Sound Garden Ideas

The secret to creating safe, diverse, and developmentally appropriate sound gardens for infants and toddlers is placing items at low heights. The inverted metal containers in this photo are at three levels, which allows access for infants, toddlers, and preschoolers. Containers may be played while sitting, kneeling, or standing. An interesting collection of pots, pans, and trays mounted low on a fence are perfect for striking with different utensils. Hold or prop up trash cans and lids while children bang on them. If an infant or toddler is sensitive to loud noises, consider adding bells and maracas. Gourds and seedpods are natural alternatives to purchased plastic maracas. Once the seeds dry inside, a wonderful shaker is created. Just ensure that any natural materials you make available are not choking or poisonous hazards, especially if infants are likely to put materials in their mouths.

Chapter 5
Mud Kitchens

Glancing over at the mud kitchen one dreary February day, I am captivated by the children's engagement and the fact that the work surface is almost hidden under mud-covered containers, damp leaves, and lots of mud. Everett (age 14 months) stares intently as he stirs his mixture quickly and continually. I wonder if his fascination is with the transformation of dirt and water, the sound of the metal spoon striking the metal bowl, or the rotating movement. Bernadette (age two) carefully scoops one spoonful of dirt at a time into a muffin tin, while Mariano (age three) transfers dirt from a tin to a pan. At the far end of the kitchen, Sebastian (age four) and Drew (age four) are focused on preparing a feast for Tyrannosaurus Rex. Perhaps T-Rex will like mini gourds to start, followed by a stone salad. The main

course is leaves in mud soup, and dessert is mud pie sprinkled with dry grass. Sebastian pours more water into a blue container as Drew mixes the soup ingredients. Drew turns from time to time and asks for more water. For the next 30 minutes, the boys focus on the task at hand. As the meal comes to an end, T-Rex wants coffee. Drew uses a wooden spoon to combine dirt and water in a red enamel camping coffeepot into a rich, dark coffee. The coffee is so thick that it will not pour into a coffee mug. Sebastian adds more water to the pot, and Drew stirs until the coffee is the perfect consistency. Every day offers exciting new possibilities in the mud kitchen.

Schema Learning

Transporting: carrying water, dirt, sand, concoctions, and loose parts

Transforming: mixing dirt and water; adding herbs, stones, and leaves

Trajectory: mashing, pounding, sprinkling, dumping, and pouring

Rotation: stirring, mixing, whisking, blending, and swirling

Enclosing/enveloping: placing loose parts inside containers; wrapping thick mud with leaves

Connecting/disconnecting: placing a lid on a pot; tearing leaves off a stem; breaking apart bark

The Value of Mud Kitchen Play

An outdoor or mud kitchen is designed for pretend cooking, mixing concoctions, experimenting, and transforming. The space contains materials for stirring, pouring, draining, measuring, and washing. Children may combine things such as dirt and water using a spoon, spatula, wire whisk, or stick and add special ingredients such as rosemary. Alexa uses a colander to drain excess liquid from sticks, which represent spaghetti. She then transfers water from one container to another as she pretends to pour sauce on top. Ari is flipping tree cookies that represent pancakes. Play in mud kitchens provides tremendous opportunities to develop imagination, initiative, critical thinking, and sustained purpose.

Mud Kitchen Play to Foster Learning

1. Enhancing Social and Emotional Competencies

Social interactions flourish in a mud kitchen as children share space and materials, form positive relationships and cooperate with other children, and take on various roles. By acting as chef or grandma, children are developing social skills and increasing their emotional understanding. Children exhibit an understanding of self, different from and related to others, as they say, "I'm making coffee just like my dad." They recognize and regulate emotions as they share pots and pans, listen to others' directions, or wait their turn for the mortar and pestle. Children become independent and competent through measuring, pouring, and mixing. Through socio-dramatic play, children develop the capacity to use objects to represent other objects, such as pretending that a pine cone is a muffin. Using one object or symbol to represent another is necessary for learning to read and write.

2. Enhancing Language and Communication Competencies

Mud kitchens are language-rich environments. Vocabulary increases as children use unusual measurement words (*dash, pinch, drop*), tool and ingredient words (*spatula, sifter, spice*), process words (*stir, flip, drain, mold*), or relationship words (*before, after, change*). There is something about being outside and combining dirt and water that encourages children to share their thoughts and talk freely about what they are doing. Language develops through descriptive words and exploration, as seen when Erika excitedly states, "Look what happened when I slapped my mushy pie!"

3. Enhancing Cognitive Competencies

Through play at a mud kitchen, children develop thinking, inquiry, and prediction skills. They recognize cause-and-effect relationships. "When I added sand, the mixture got thick and made it harder to stir." Children learn to predict outcomes. "If I add more water, the mixture will become soupy." Mud kitchens are science-rich environments for children to engage, notice, wonder, and question. Scientific inquiry expands as children transform, transfer, and transport materials in an open-ended way. Exploration in a mud kitchen promotes mathematical concepts such as comparison, measurement, classification, spatial relationships, and one-to-one correspondence. For example, spoons are made from different materials (metal and wood), and come in different designs (slotted, ladle, rice) and sizes (miniature, small, big). Children develop an understanding of measurement as they fill containers or pour cups of water into a larger container. Spatial relationships develop as children reach out to grasp a wooden spoon and know how far to stretch or place materials in front of, underneath, above, beside, or inside. One-to-one correspondence is evident when Brady puts one spoon in each container.

4. Enhancing Physical Competencies

Children increase small motor skills and coordination by pouring, mixing, mashing, grinding, beating, and sifting. Children's hand muscles strengthen as they grasp spatulas and spoons and carry heavy pots of dirt or water. Wet dirt takes strength to carry and handle. Manipulation and eye-hand coordination improve as a child flips up the spigot on a water dispenser or takes dirt out of a mixing bowl with an ice scoop. Bilateral coordination, the ability to use both sides of the body at the same time, advances as Sean pushes a rolling pin with both his hands and Rita holds the pan handle with her right hand while stirring the mixture with her left hand.

5. Enhancing Expressive Arts

Children's imaginations thrive as they respond to the interesting materials and exciting possibilities. Creativity abounds as children elaborate and extend their thoughts and ideas. Mud in a pie pan becomes a birthday cake topped with sticks for candles. Grass, seashells, and leaves are sautéed to create a delicious pad Thai. Creative chefs improvise, put together ingredients in new ways, and push culinary boundaries—in the mud kitchen as in real kitchens. The materials and space provide a platform for children to make sense of imaginary, abstract, or real-life experiences by dramatizing an event over and over.

Essential Components: What Every Mud Kitchen Needs

Space: A mud kitchen works well on level ground along a fence or building or under a tree, awning, canopy, or pergola for protection on hot and wet days. Work in the space can be messy, so select a low-maintenance, easy-to-clean ground surface such as concrete, play yard bark, pavers, or crushed rock. Avoid grass, as excessive use and spilled dirt and sand will destroy it.

Work space: Think of your own kitchen at home and how frustrating it is when you do not have enough room to place bowls and ingredients on the counter. Consider what it is like when you have family or friends over and multiple people are using the kitchen at the same time. It becomes very crowded and challenging for everyone to work. The same is true for a mud kitchen: more space is welcomed.

Mud kitchens with the most charm and character are made from found and donated items. A work surface can be as simple as a wooden bench or wide wood plank on top of two crates or tree trunks. As in your own kitchen, the work happens standing up. A play oven, stove top, or sink are not necessary and take up valuable work space. Instead, a clear, open surface provides more flexibility and requires more creativity.

An optimal work space size is 8 feet in length, 2 feet in width, and 18 to 24 inches in height, depending on the age of the children. More children and heavy usage demand additional space. Extend the space by adding benches or other work surfaces to create a U shape, or add another level, such as storage shelves or hooks mounted on a fence or lattice to hold pots and pans.

Outdoor furniture must be durable; redwood, cedar, teak, and acacia are hardy choices and have beautiful color tones. Commercial patio benches and tables can be found in teak and acacia. Redwood has an element inside the pores that makes it weather-, insect-, and rot-resistant, lasting longer than other woods when exposed to the elements. All wood discolors over time, particularly with heavy sun exposure. Reseal the wood once a year as part of regular maintenance. To refinish, lightly sand the entire surface. Any remaining finish need not be removed. Then, following the manufacturer's instructions, apply one or two coats of an eco-friendly, nontoxic exterior wood sealer, such as a soy-based product. Seek advice from an expert at a local hardware store if uncertain. Mud kitchens may be covered with a tarp or barbecue cover for protection against the rain and snow.

Mud kitchen before

Mud kitchen after

This mud kitchen area had great potential. There was beautiful wooden furniture for work surfaces, but a pink plastic house dominated the space. The ground surface consisted of large rubber tiles covered in a dusting of sand. Cooking utensils were scattered, and the space was cluttered with too much furniture. There was no clear message about what to do in the space or where to find materials.

Underneath the sandy rubber tiles, we discovered a foundation of beautiful red stone pavers. We removed the rubber tiles and hosed off the stone pavers. The result was a stunning tile floor. The pink house was taken away, the wooden benches relocated, and the wooden work surfaces repositioned. A small table was added for preparing or serving food. Authentic kitchen utensils are now organized in convenient, accessible containers on countertops. Children can access water from water jugs with spigots and find dirt in galvanized tubs. Canisters are filled with natural loose parts of pine cones, tree cookies, and cinnamon sticks to extend children's play.

Enhancing mud kitchens: Appealing mud kitchens have authenticity, simplicity, texture, and emphasis. Begin with furniture constructed from wood. Whether pallets, benches, or child-sized countertops, furniture and work surfaces made of wood offer genuineness. Wood provides a warm, beautiful, and realistic look. A plastic children's toy kitchen set may be cute, but it can be visually overwhelming with gadgets and bright colors. Wood tones blend in with natural surroundings. Place real wood and metal tools of varying sizes in a galvanized canister, ceramic crock, or farmhouse pitcher. An uncluttered space that reveals simplicity is beautiful. This can be achieved by organizing like materials together and displaying only important items. Having too many items in too little space interferes with aesthetics. Vary texture and add color through materials, plants, and surfaces. Add herbs growing in terra-cotta pots on the work surface: parsley, sage, rosemary, and thyme. A red enamel coffee pot and mugs add vintage flair and a splash of color. A ground surface of brick pavers or teak flooring adds allure and appeal to the senses.

Mud Kitchen Tools and Materials

When selecting items for the space, consider preparing, measuring, and baking tools that are found in your own kitchen. Children prefer to play with real kitchen items and not imitations. Select items that are stainless or galvanized steel to avoid rust. Thrift stores and garage sales are excellent places to find pots and pans. Some baking items, such as pie, cake, and bread pans, can be purchased inexpensively at discount stores. These items will hold up for a season and then will need to be replaced because of rust. Replenish rusted and broken materials on a rotating basis as part of maintenance.

Dirt: Dirt is the primary ingredient of a mud kitchen. Other substances such as sand can be added. Use topsoil found in garden stores for filling holes and leveling low areas. Read the ingredient list on packages carefully and avoid any dirt that contains fertilizer. Store dirt in a large galvanized tub next to or under the work surface. Place additional dirt in canisters or large bowls on top of the workstation.

Water source: Every mud kitchen needs water. Use clear and never colored water, as cooking is always done with clear water. If a permanent water source is not available, bowls or pitchers of water may be set on top of the work surface, or use plastic water jugs with spigots. This allows children to independently access the water they need. Place metal cream pitchers or tin cans next to the water and encourage children to get just the amount they need at a time. Adults can refill water jugs when empty or have children participate in refilling with adult supervision. Always assist children in the refill process, as dirt poured into a water jug clogs and destroys the spigot.

Kitchenware
Bread pans
Cake pans
Canisters
Colanders
Mixing bowls
Mortar and pestle
Muffin tins
Pie pans
Skillets and saucepans
Small metal creamer
   pitchers
Strainers
Tin cans

Utensils
Metal spoons
Pancake turners
Potato mashers
Slotted spoons
Spatulas
Wire whisks
Wooden spoons

Herbs and natural materials extend mud kitchen play.

Water containers with spigots allow children to access water on their own.

Storage and Organization

Cooking materials need to be organized within easy reach. Utensils can be placed in a bucket, utensil caddy, tin can, or pitcher. Consider vertical organizers such as a mounted towel bar or metal basket on the side of the mud kitchen to hang utensils, or install a pegboard or open wood frame (lattice, trellis) behind or next to the work space. Fences can offer the perfect vertical space to hang tools or pots and pans. Hang them from a suspended ladder or high shelf or use benches and shelving units to store materials.

Using vertical storage to hang pots and pans creates more work surface space.

Cleaning and Maintaining the Space

Just as with your kitchen at home, it is hard to work in a space that is overwhelmed with clutter. Taking a few minutes daily to arrange and combine items will prepare the play space for next time. If there is a place for everything, then everything can easily go back to its place. You do not need to be meticulous—just tidy—to create order. Replenish dirt, water, and accessory materials so that they are ready for the next play session. If the mud kitchen is not under cover, store items upside down so water does not accumulate inside. Provide a whisk broom and dustpan for sweeping up dirt. For easy cleanup, purchase a lightweight cordless leaf blower. At the end of the day, you can simply blow off excess dirt. Materials will need to be hosed off periodically. Children can help rinse off items if a large tub of water is available at cleanup time. Check items for rust and breakage, and replace as needed.

The Extra Dimension

Creating mixtures with pots, pans, dirt, and water is very satisfying for children. Adding small loose parts can further enhance the space, extend interest, and deepen play. Have supplies of natural loose parts available in small containers on the work surface. Know too that children will instinctively collect natural items from around the yard, such as grass, leaves, acorns, or liquid amber tree or sweetgum tree balls. Consider placing pots of herbs on the work surface. They add both beauty and play potential. Herbs can be picked and ground in a mortar and pestle and then added

as a special ingredient to concoctions. Herbs are a safe option, as they are nontoxic. Flowers or other plants may be used, but always check to make certain that they are safe for children. Consider including these extras:

- Bark
- Cinnamon sticks
- Herbs: rosemary, thyme, sage, basil, mint, oregano
- Leaves
- Seashells
- Small pine cones
- Stones
- Tree cookies
- Twigs

Supporting Equitable Learning

- Use loose parts for children to create food that is part of their own family culture.
- Avoid plastic food, as it is limiting and can be stereotypic. Loose parts may be used to represent anything.
- Avoid using real food, as this is disrespectful to children who experience food insecurity and confusing for children taught not to play with food.
- Provide water sources, such as jugs with spigots, that children can independently access.
- Offer kitchen utensils with varying grips for children who have weak grasps or limited arm movement.

Old benches provide additional work space.

Camping enamelware is a durable choice for mud kitchens.

Infant/Toddler Mud Kitchen Ideas

Toddlers love to fill, pour, and mix in mud kitchens. Simple containers and spoons along with a bit of dirt and water are all that is needed. Adaptations from traditional mud kitchens are unnecessary unless you want to lower the work surface to 18 inches, which is standard toddler height. The mud kitchens I place in mixed-age programs are 20 inches, and even infants can pull themselves up and engage with materials at this height. A low platform or tree stump can be placed next to the mud kitchen if a child wants to be taller. When adding loose parts such as stones or pine cones, make sure that they are not a choking hazard.

Chapter 6
Small Worlds

A land of snow and ice captures the attention of Everett (14 months) and Alexa (age three). A white scarf simulates a thick layer of snow, a beautiful textured piece of birch bark represents an irresistible icy hill, and a black piece of slate evokes the deep ocean water. Birch tree blocks, figurines of polar bears from the Arctic, and penguins from Antarctica make up the props. Alexa's story line includes a penguin who dives off a birch block into icy cold water to be with her penguin family. She then lays the penguin on its stomach and toboggans it down the icy birch bark slide. After Alexa leaves, Everett uses his hands to move around the table. As he places a penguin on top of a birch block, the block tumbles off the table into the bark below. He picks up the block and reaches to place a penguin on top of it in midair. He relocates the block onto the table and steadies it before placing a penguin on top. For several minutes, he retrieves birch blocks that topple to the ground as he works to place penguins on top of each one. His persistence and focus for engaging with the small world materials are impressive. He demonstrates one-to-one correspondence as he places one penguin on top of each block. Three birch blocks and four penguins on the table present a challenge. Everett removes a penguin from atop a block and replaces it with another. Then he pauses, puts down the penguin in his hand, grasps the polar bear, and totters away.

The Value of Small Worlds

Small worlds are an imaginative experience for children that involves miniature playscapes and promotes dramatic play. They are a valuable aspect of role play, encouraging children to expand their imaginations. Teachers create play settings based on observation and their understanding of children's interests. Teachers and children add characters and accessories or change the setting as the children's interests, needs, and experiences with an environment evolve. Small worlds are usually designed around a theme such as fairies, dinosaurs, or construction, or are framed around a habitat such as an ocean or forest, the four seasons, or a familiar story. Adding loose parts, small props, and sensory elements such as sand, dirt, water, or gravel to a small world expands and extends the complexity of children's outdoor play.

> ### Schema Learning
>
> **Transporting:** carrying or moving props to and from the small world
>
> **Transforming:** changing the arrangement of materials in the playscape
>
> **Enclosing:** building a boundary around small-world props; creating a fence, wall, barricade, or hedge
>
> **Enveloping:** hiding or covering up small-world props
>
> **Connecting/disconnecting:** attaching loose parts together; taking the small world apart

Small-World Play to Foster Learning

1. Enhancing Social and Emotional Competencies

Emotional development is promoted through small-world play as children process and act out their feelings, understandings, concerns, and life events. The play provides similar benefits as fantasy or imaginative play but in small, portable spaces. Children can reenact experiences, investigate emotions, and experiment with themes of mastery and control in a safe, secure way. They are free to cope with troubling, exciting, and enjoyable situations at their own developmental level. They can spend long periods of time setting up a fire scene, fairy kingdom, or reptile world while narrating their ideas out loud. This play allows children to adjust their behavior responses to circumstances, clarify ideas and concepts, address life's difficult challenges, and regain a sense of control when they feel powerless.

Most important, small-world play can assist children in processing life circumstances such as birth of a sibling, illness, abandonment, divorce, and death. Mia has been struggling with the recent separation of her parents. She is unaware of her dad's substance abuse challenges and confused as to why her dad has moved out. Observing Mia's play, the teachers take note that she is anxious about not going on the family's annual camping trip. Going camping was a favorite time that she shared with her dad. They talk with Mia's mom and learn that the camping trip is still happening even though Mia's dad will not be coming. They agree that setting up a camping small world may help Mia process her feelings in preparation for the trip. Throughout the next days, the teachers observe how Mia's engagement with the camping small world allows her to express her joy of going camping, handle the difficult emotions of her dad not being present, and acquire a sense of control over a stressful situation.

Small-world play supports children's social development as children work collaboratively, share, take turns, solve problems, and learn to respect the ideas of others. As children manipulate loose parts as characters, they learn how to interact socially and develop social cues by experimenting with eye contact, using different tones of voice, and expressing emotions. Through the pretend play, children discover who they are separate from others and explore their place in the world. Compromise and negotiation happen as children consider how to arrange a habitat and determine how a play scenario will unfold. Relationships are formed, and children share responsibility reenacting stories alongside each other.

2. Enhancing Language and Communication Competencies

It is captivating to listen in as children engage in small-world play. Their language can be humorous, eye-popping, and revealing as they use words or expressions that we were unaware they knew. Sometimes the words hit too close to home as we recognize the phrases or tone as our own. Small-world play is wonderful for developing children's language, communication, and literacy competencies because it allows children to practice language in a meaningful context. As children tinker with language, they discover the power of words. They learn that language can express ideas or feelings, argue a point, convey information, evoke a response (for example, *persuade* or *entertain*), and initiate or maintain contact with people. Children begin to connect language, objects, and actions to create increasingly complex story lines and adapt their language to reflect different perspectives and roles. They experiment with the language of possession and position and learn about nouns, verbs, and adjectives, as when placing a starfish on top of light blue pebbles and next to white sea glass. Small-world play also encourages children to extend stories from books. For example, children can play with a small-world pond to retell or alter the story *Mossy* by Jan Brett. They can reflect on what interests them and express their feelings about the story.

3. Enhancing Cognitive Competencies

Children's concept development is promoted through problem solving and inquiry as they play with small worlds. Acquiring a concept begins with concrete experiences with real objects. Small worlds contain real things to explore and manipulate, such as stones, sticks, plants, seashells, sand, and bark. As children engage with these concrete materials, their play includes themes and situations that require problem solving. Children learn how to solve challenges through experimenting and reasoning. They might figure out how to make a slide for penguins, construct a bridge for the "Three Billy Goats Gruff," or arrange tree blocks to enclose a watering hole for elephants. Small-world characters face problems that require solutions, such as getting hurt or lost or dealing with monsters and bad guys. As Grace, Mackenzie, and Dayton explore an "On the Moon" small world, they encounter problems, including crashing, running out of gas, and unfriendly aliens.

Small-world play provides children with the context to expand their understanding of the world. Play with small worlds is rich in possibilities for learning about familiar places and unknown habitats, such as the forest, arctic, ocean, and jungle. The size of small worlds permits children to explore habitats that would be impossible to re-create on a larger scale. For example, after Erika went on a nature hike with her family, she shared her experience at school. The teachers simulated a forest small world with a variety of natural loose parts, including pine cones, evergreen branches, and figurines of forest animals for Erika and other children to make links between their play world and a real forest.

As young children explore small worlds, several fundamental mathematical concepts are naturally exhibited in their play, including problem-solving abilities, reasoning, and understanding of numeracy concepts. Take Gabriel, Mateo, and Ivy, who help set up a farm small world in a redwood planter box with farmyard animal figures, grass, dirt, and recycled materials. They separate the space into two areas by placing grass on one side and dirt on the other. Next, using loose parts, they create smaller sections for the farmhouse, barn, duck pond, corral, pigpen, and field (investigating part/whole relations and shapes). They place props inside, under, on top of, or next to each other (understanding space and position). Farmyard animal figures are sorted into groups (practicing classification). Cows are placed on the grass, pigs in a dirt pen, ducks on an unbreakable mirror for a pond, and horses in a corral. Gabriel adds water to the dirt pen, and pigs begin to roll in the mud. Soon there are clean pigs and dirty pigs (making comparisons). The muddy pigs need a bath. Meanwhile, Ivy divides the corral with sticks to make horse stalls and places one horse in each stall (showing one-to-one correspondence). Later she lines up horses from small to large (practicing seriation). Mateo uses trial and error to make miniature bricks fit in a rectangle shape for a cornfield (practicing measurement).

Skylar and Hazel show their ability to add and subtract while playing with a butterfly fairy garden. Skylar hands a fairy to Hazel: "Here, now you have one and I have one." Hazel giggles, "Wait, this one was hiding. Oh no, here's another guarding the fairy dust." She adds two fairies to their collection and announces, "Now we have four!" "Yeah, now we have four!" repeats Skylar. Hazel says, "If she hides again, we'll only have three" (practicing subtraction). Hazel creates a path to the fairy dust stash by alternating blue and white glass stones (exploring patterning). Skylar positions a fairy on the very top of the burl: "Look, she's the tallest fairy of all!" (practicing measurement).

4. Enhancing Physical Competencies

Small worlds provide children with opportunity to develop perceptual motor and small-motor skills. Perceptual motor skills integrate the senses (perceptual skills) and motor abilities. As children interact with a small world, they increase body awareness, spatial awareness, and directional awareness. For example, Liam positions his body to kneel next to the forest small world to manipulate the twigs, pine cones, and bears. Elijah reaches for a stone that represents an egg in the dragon's lair small world without knocking over the sleeping dragon. And Benjamin uses his arms to push and mold kinetic sand into sandcastles in the beach life environment. Hand-eye coordination and fine motor skills are refined as children manipulate natural materials and a range of small-world props. While playing with a winter small world, Adalee pinches a clear glass stone between her finger and thumb in her left hand and grasps a smooth metal S hook with her full right fist. Next she shifts her attention to the pure white sand, which represents snow. She experiences tactile and visual sensory stimulation as she rubs her hand across the smooth, soft sand and grasps and rotates a hard blue agate coaster with banded patterns. Ensley steadies a basket of stones on her lap. Carefully she takes stones from the basket with one hand while holding the container with other hand (bimanual dexterity) and places them in a pile.

5. Enhancing Expressive Arts

Small-world play absorbs children in a creative endeavor. The value of small worlds is evident when children allow their imaginations full rein and express their interests, fascinations, thoughts, feelings, and sometimes concerns. The openness of the materials allows children to explore freely. Their imaginations can turn an acorn cap into a hat, a seashell into a pond, or bark into dragon's food. Play with small worlds involves fantasy, imagination, and make-believe, all creative behaviors. Children create real-life and imaginary scenarios and explore situations and personal experiences. Play with a small world is spontaneous; it is not practiced or planned. Children make up a story in the moment that can go in unknown directions. The plot unfolds as children use items in the small world to symbolize people and objects. Children take on roles of characters and determine the action. Often there is a struggle or problem that needs to be resolved, such as protection from danger, finding something, or completing a task. Dinosaurs may need safety from an erupting volcano, a bunny may need to find his family, or a bridge may need rebuilding after a flood. The story can be simple or elaborate. In each case, the situations lead to interesting and sometimes unexpected results.

Essential Components: What Every Small World Needs

Space: Small worlds can be created anywhere outdoors. A permanent location may be used, such as a flower bed, repurposed tree stump, redwood planter box, fountain, or hollow log. Small worlds can also be designed in portable containers, such as an old wheelbarrow or tire. (See page 176 for more information about safely repurposing old tires.) They may be tucked in a corner; nestled into existing landscaping; situated on a tabletop, bench, deck, or patio; or positioned in sun or shade. Wherever you decide, place the small world away from traffic in a quiet location and consider how children will reach and manipulate materials. Its placement and physical arrangement will send a message to children: Is this a secluded space where children can be solo or with a friend without intrusion, or is this a space for several children to reenact a story, socialize, and play from different vantage points?

Small world before

This redwood planter was once filled with plants to decorate the play yard. All but one plant has died, leaving the planter bare and full of potential.

Small world after

Teacher Cheri decided to transform the planter box in the yard of her family child care into a small world. She selected the savanna as the theme because of the children's recent interest in zebras and giraffes. She created ground surfaces with sand, rocks, and wood and designed a river with small pebbles to meander through the middle of the box. Zebras can graze on the grassland while the hippopotamuses live in the slow-moving river. The existing fern is perfect for giraffes to reach up and eat the high leaves and shoots.

> **Top Tips for Designing Small Worlds**
>
> 1. Locate it in a quiet space away from traffic.
> 2. Arrange it in a container.
> 3. Base it around a theme.
> 4. Design it in layers—soil, plants, surfaces, and accessories. Begin with the biggest pieces and save the smaller ones until the end. Place larger items in the back and smaller items to the front.
> 5. Make the surface from natural materials that are aesthetically pleasing.
> 6. Use natural loose parts and small figurines as props.

Theme: When creating a small world, the first thing to start with is the theme or habitat. Think of the habitat as a community where people or animals share the same place, interest, or action. Understanding children's interests, fascinations, concerns, energy, and eagerness for adventure will serve as a guide for selecting a theme. Here are some examples:

Fantasy habitats: fairies, gnomes, unicorns, dragons, trolls
Adventure habitats: space, pirates, dinosaurs, volcano, cave
Naturalist habitats: wetlands, forests, grasslands, tundra, oceans, jungle, deserts, tide pool, beach
Aquatic habitats: pond, marsh, river, stream, lake, ocean
Animal habitats: insects, worms, reptiles, birds, mice
Literature and fairy tales: *Mossy*, "The Three Billy Goats Gruff," "The Three Little Pigs"
Season habitats: spring, summer, fall, winter
Action habitats: trains, cars, trucks, building site, excavating site
Daily living habitats: dollhouses, picnic, tea party, city, farm, apartment, house

Small-World Tools and Materials

Containers and bases: Just about anything can be transformed into a container for a small world. This is the perfect time to upcycle and be creative in repurposing and reusing old things. Use your imagination to turn an old planter, galvanized tub, dresser drawer, hat, birdbath, or vintage suitcase into an intriguing container. Small worlds can be made on flat surfaces such as a rug, piece of tile, or wood plank if the accessory pieces do not need to be contained. Use a container with depth, such as a boot tray for playscapes that have sand, dirt, pebbles, or materials that need to be enclosed. One advantage of using a tray is that the small world is portable. If the small world will contain plants, it is important for the container to have good drainage. Select wooden or ceramic planters designed for outdoors, or drill holes in the chosen container to give adequate drainage.

Barrel	Cookie sheet	Rug
Bathtub	Drawer	Serving tray
Birdbath	Flowerpot saucer	Sheet pan
Boot tray	Gravel pan	Suitcase
Box lid	Hollow log	Tire
Builder tray	Jelly roll pan	Wagon
Burl wood or large log	Mud tray	Wheelbarrow
Clay saucers	Oil pan	Window boxes
Colander	Planter	Wood tray
Concrete mixing tub	Raised garden bed	Wooden barrel
	Redwood planter box	

Small-world plants: The colors and textures of plants bring a wonderful aesthetic to a small world. They add focal points and hiding places and provide interest and unity. Plants also connect children to the natural world. The best plants for a small world are herbs, as they are edible, can be grown in any well-drained soil, and do not require a lot of care, although they require high levels of sunlight. Some flowering herbs such as chives and rosemary may attract bees if not trimmed. Succulents are another good option if they have smooth leaves and stems. They are hardy and thrive in dry conditions. Most succulents are not toxic to humans. Always seek advice from a master gardener to ensure that you select only safe plants for children and choose the best plants for your climate zone and specific problem situations. Plants in permanent containers can be replaced in different seasons. For example, strawberries can be added in springtime, flowers in the summer, a picked pumpkin in the fall, or evergreens in the winter. Plants should be well established before allowing children to play with the small world.

Basil	Oregano	Strawberries
Chives	Parsley	Succulents
Cilantro	Peppermint	Sweet marjoram
Dill	Rosemary	Tarragon
Mint	Sage	Thyme

Small-world accessories: Look for props and natural materials that are part of the habitat's community. For example, a forest playscape needs forest inhabitants, such as squirrels, rabbits, beavers, racoons, deer, foxes, and bears. Natural materials include pine cones, tree bark, branches, twigs, leaves, and small rocks. Anything in nature can become part of a small world. Good small worlds must have plenty of open-ended materials available to extend imaginative play. For instance, twigs may be used to make a beaver dam or fishing poles. Bark may be transformed into a tent, or stones may make a bear cave. Surfaces such as moss, dirt, and sand form the foundation of the landscape. Dried, crushed herbs make great pathways and add sensory appeal.

Small-World Surfaces

Bark
Basil leaves (dried)
Cocoa mulch
Coconut husk bedding
Corncob bedding
Dill weed (dried)
Dirt
Eucalyptus leaves
   (dried)
Flowering kale
Forest moss
Glass stones
Gravel
Hay
Kinetic sand
Lavender (dried)
Mint (dried)
Moss
Pebbles
Reindeer moss
Rosebuds (dried)
Rosemary (dried)
Sheet moss
Sod
Spanish moss (dried)
Spearmint (dried)
Straw
Wheatgrass

Small-World Loose Parts

Acorns
Branches
Cinnamon sticks
Driftwood
Eucalyptus pods
Leaves
Pine cones
Scarves
Sea beans
Sea glass
Seashells
Seedpods
Spools (wooden)
Sticks
Stones
Tiles
Tree cookies
Twigs
White mulberry
   root bark

Plants added to playscapes provide texture, color, and beauty.

Cocoa mulch offers an intriguing sensory experience while children engage with this farm small world.

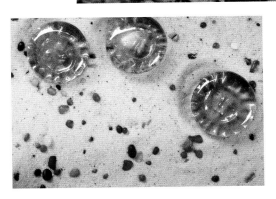

Design and Assembly

Once the container, inhabitants, props, loose parts, and surfaces have been gathered, it is time to design the small world. A good starting point is to design in layers—soil, plants, surfaces, then accessories. Consider sketching a layout ahead of time, especially when re-creating a familiar scene. For example, for the "Three Little Pigs," the three houses need to be spread apart with a pathway connecting them. Begin with the biggest pieces and save the smaller ones until the end. Place larger items in the back and smaller items in the front. For permanent playscapes that will have plants, begin by filling the container with dirt and arranging plants as desired. For portable playscapes, begin with surface materials such as kinetic sand and moss, followed by larger props. The final touches include stepping-stones, pathways, loose parts, and inhabitants. Remember that less is best when starting out, and simplicity is key. Include only one sensory element and a couple of props in initial small worlds. Add accessories and sensory elements when children are ready for more complexity.

Storage and Organization

Generally, accessories and props for small worlds are contained in the small world, so there is no need for extra storage. Additional props may be set out on the table or floor next to the playscape. Small worlds containing absorbent materials like scarves or corncob bedding need to be protected or taken inside during inclement weather. Corncob bedding swells up and can become moldy when wet.

Cleaning and Maintaining the Space

Small worlds need to be straightened and rearranged after use. Materials may need to be replaced and new items added to extend children's play. It takes just a few minutes to restage surfaces and props. For instance, a stone pathway may need to be re-created, moss tucked under a log, or washers placed back in a pie tin. A tip for retrieving smaller pieces from finer surfaces such as sand is to use a wire sifter or berry basket to scoop up items and then shake. A tidy small world gives the message, "Come play with me, and here are the available props," while a messy world says, "Someone else is playing or has played here." Children do not know what to do when things are messy. Think of your own home when clutter takes over. It can be hard to focus and know where to begin when you cannot find the tools you need.

A word of caution: If you are a person who is not fond of mess and likes order, I encourage you to select small-world materials carefully and use a limited number of items. Know that children will mix materials, so if you do not want sand poured into water, consider using an acrylic mirror instead of water. If you do not want crushed spearmint and oregano to mix, use only one dried herb.

Small worlds may need adjustments to support children's play. Carefully listen to their language and observe their actions. You may discover that children need more room to maneuver around the small world, that attention is dwindling and a location change may be helpful, or that there are too many or too few materials.

The Extra Dimension

Creating small worlds is contagious. You will find tremendous delight in discovering unique containers and designing imaginative playscapes. Think literally out of the box when selecting materials to represent objects. For example, a scarf, sand, or blue glass gems make perfect "water." An acrylic mirror is good for a pond or ice. Sprinkling crushed colored gems into white sand gives a magical feel to a fairy garden. Small birdhouses can be covered in straw, sticks, and stones to make homes for the three little pigs. A pathway sprinkled with dried rosemary or rose petals adds striking color and aromas. Explore many possibilities for creating unique and imaginative small worlds.

Supporting Equitable Learning

- Let children use materials in ways that are most meaningful to them.
- Give children control of their make-believe play.
- Resist temptation to impose order on children's pretend play.
- Avoid using food products in small-world landscapes, as this is disrespectful for children who do not have enough food at home and confusing for children taught not to play with food.
- Limit the number of props, as too much is worse than too little for some children.
- Support children in entering small-world play and maintaining group membership.
- Encourage children to talk about concerns in their lives, and set up small worlds that allow children to reenact situations from their lives.
- Help children who do not pretend-play well to learn how to do so.
- Place small worlds at different levels so all children have access.

Cinnamon sticks become logs in this construction small world.

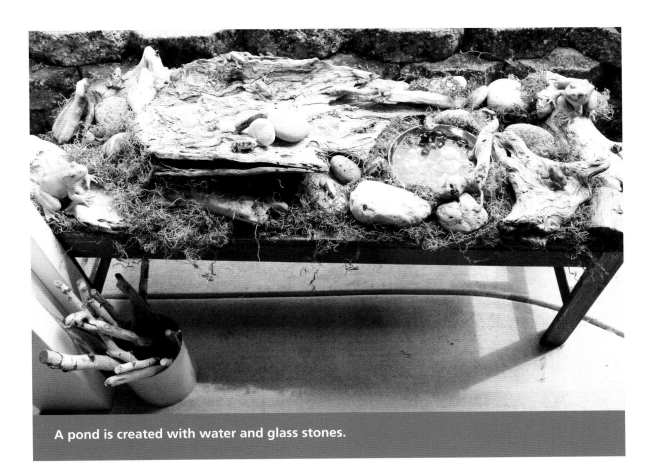

A pond is created with water and glass stones.

Children helped make the houses for the three little pigs.

Infant/Toddler Small-World Ideas

Infant and toddler small-world play is about discovery: What are these materials? What are their most interesting properties? What can I do with them? Small worlds may be modified for younger children by using larger props, such as extra-large frogs or extra-large bugs in a pond small-world habitat. Replace loose parts with larger pieces that are not choking hazards. Know that infants and toddlers will grasp, mix, and drop materials. Consider your mess tolerance and avoid problems by limiting materials and simplifying the playscape. For example, a modified bunny small world could include a green rug with cuddly toy bunnies and a carpet tube peeking out from under the rug as a rabbit burrow. A duck pond could consist of a blue scarf, carpet square, or strips of fabric to form a pond and toy ducks.

Chapter 7
Construction Zones

Today the construction zone is being transformed into a large home for children to go in with the design expertise of Charlie (age five), Bernadette (age two), and Diana (age three). The floor plan unfolds as the girls use big construction zone loose parts. Working with the materials requires an understanding of balance, stability, and function. First comes a dining room table made with a large wooden wire cable spool. Four smaller wire cable spools become chairs. Spools and planks form bedroom walls, followed by a medium bed and a small bed. Diana reports, "The dog is not allowed to sleep in the cat bed." It is unclear whether the bedroom is for people or pets. With a wooden crate, Bernadette creates a bathroom that opens to the dining room. This location may not be ideal in a house, but its placement demonstrates that it is a high priority for preschoolers. Eating is also important, so the girls put a lot of effort into counter space for food. Shelves are constructed with what Diana calls "horsey walkers" (sawhorses), crates, and planks.

Tree cookies and driftwood pieces become essential food: watermelon, pink fishy crackers, and apples. Later the floor plan is modified by the in-house designers when Charlie announces, "We need to make another bedroom" and "Our living room needs to be bigger." Making and changing the floor plan involves a lot of decision-making and critical thinking as the girls create a flow between spaces. Furniture and walls can easily be moved and a space turned into something else. Having the opportunity and flexibility to design spaces is powerful for children as they explore their own abilities, understanding, creativity, and mastery with large loose parts.

Schema Learning

Transporting: moving and carrying building materials; using pulleys

Transforming: creating structures from building materials

Trajectory: building inclines with wood planks

Rotation: rotating wooden spools

Enclosing/enveloping: building structures around self or enclosures for play animals

Connecting/disconnecting: hooking pipes together and taking them apart

The Value of Construction Zones

Blocks are one of the most fundamental, versatile, enjoyable, and essential materials used in early childhood programs. There is no better material than blocks for igniting innovation, imagination, and creativity. An outdoor construction zone has all the same elements for building real and imaginary structures and testing like a mechanical or civil engineer but on a larger scale than indoors, and includes a wide variety of large, open-ended construction materials. Noise and mess are not an issue, and young builders can practice risk-taking. In addition, structures often can be left up so that day after day children can expand upon their work. In this exciting environment designed for building and engineering, children are free to eagerly investigate, probe, and experiment. Since construction materials are open-ended, there are infinite play possibilities for a child.

Construction Zones to Foster Learning

1. Enhancing Social and Emotional Competencies

Construction materials are ideal for fostering self-esteem, competence, and independence as children take risks and make decisions. Increasing self-confidence is revealed in children's smiles and exuberant pride as they successfully build a tall tower. As children construct with materials, they act independently, processing challenges, feeling capable, and learning from their interactions and experiences with others. Sebastian's tongue protrudes as he stretches far above his head to add a fifth redwood block to his tower. He steps back and beams with pride as he describes his accomplishment to Alexa. The two discuss how to make it even taller. Self-regulation develops as children exert self-control and resist impulses to strike out when someone knocks down their work. Being in charge is extremely satisfying and elicits a sense of accomplishment and self-worth.

A construction zone offers social opportunities for children to cooperate, communicate, and problem solve as they build. When collaborating on building a structure such as a fort, children must negotiate and work through problems and disagreements that arise. What materials will we use? How high will the fort be? How do we keep it from toppling over?

Will there be windows? How will we keep people from getting inside our fort? Sharing materials and space encourages children to respect the work of others and cultivates the ability to empathize. As children co-construct, they share ideas and insights, learn from more accomplished builders, make friendships, persevere with frustrating tasks, and look at the world from other points of view.

2. Enhancing Language and Communication Competencies

As children construct alongside or with others, they naturally talk about their actions, plans, and needs. They share story lines about their structures, exchange ideas, and learn how to compromise. Children understand language as a social tool as they build on others' comments, clarify meaning, inform others, and express opinions and feelings. Children learn new vocabulary related to construction, such as *ramp*, *level*, *extension*, and *stable*, and physics terms such as *balance*, *distance*, *speed*, *impact*, and *projectile*. Spatial language is promoted as children recognize objects in different orientations. Children learn words describing location or position (*above*, *beside*), attributes (*short*, *high*, *long*, *symmetrical*), orientation and mental rotation (*turn*, *right*), and geometric shape names (*square*, *rectangle*, *cylinder*). Play in a construction zone is also beneficial for bilingual and nonverbal children, as it allows them to communicate their ideas in multiple ways with open-ended materials. One day Diana and Salvador build a bridge together with a large wooden crate on one end and a shallow wooden crate 8 feet away. In between the crates they line up six bed risers. A wood plank bridges the space between a riser and the large crate. The two children walk to the material storage area. Salvador says, "A big board can help." He selects a 4-foot plank and uses it to span the shallow crate and risers. He adjusts the board to center it more. Diana approaches with a 2-foot board, saying, "Yeah, and we need this." As she bends to place the plank on top of the bed risers, Salvador gestures above the risers and says, "No, Diana, we already got all the pieces we need." Diana playfully drops the plank on top of the bed risers. Salvador picks it up and hands it to Diana. "That's not a good idea. Put it away." Diana giggles, takes the plank, and returns it to the storage area. Salvador says, "Now we wreck the bridge and build a new bridge." He kicks a riser. Diana returns and follows his lead by also kicking a riser. "Yeah." The structure collapses. Salvador says, "Now, let's build a new bridge." They place the risers next to each other. As Diana holds the 4-foot plank to bridge the wooden crate and risers, Salvador pushes the two risers closer to the crate. They add three more risers to the line. Salvador steps up onto the bridge, and as he begins to walk across, the plank wobbles underneath his weight. Diana says, "Be careful." He gains his balance and continues across the bridge. He lunges forward, and then the far plank collapses underneath him as he stretches for the crate, pulls himself up, and stands on top of the crate. "I broke the bridge." Diana shouts, "I can fix it." She positions risers and planks back into position. Once again, she adds the shorter plank that Salvador does not want, and he removes it.

3. Enhancing Cognitive Competencies

Children's cognitive processes increase as they manipulate materials and encounter challenges in the construction zone. Children use logical thought and reasoning skills as they investigate different building materials. When children use wood scraps to construct towers, roads, enclosures, and bridges, they measure, estimate, and evaluate spatial relationships as they place pieces under, on top of, next to, and below. Each time children revisit materials, they apply their knowledge and understanding from previous experiences. For example, Oliver, Salvador, and Drew construct a train with crates and wood planks. When Drew discovers that wood planks can slide through the crate's slats, the structure transforms into a helicopter. Salvador says, "Look, it's the rotor!" Subsequent building includes planks in slats as the children use their earlier knowledge.

As children build progressively complex structures, they gain a deeper understanding of science concepts such as stability, gravity, and balance. Like scientists, children develop hypotheses, try them out, and experiment with materials through trial and error. This is seen as Oliver (age two) repeatedly pushes a toy car down a plank that he props against a shallow crate. Salvador (age three) drives a large metal dump truck across an obstacle course of planks and then pushes it down ramps from a tree trunk and different crates. Salvador articulates his theory to Oliver: "The high ramp makes the truck go faster." He has made a cause-and-effect connection. Later he guides Oliver in how to make the trucks go faster down his ramp.

Symbolic representation increases as children engage with loose parts in the construction zone. Mariano is building a house in the construction zone. He clutches a plank of wood under his right arm and holds out a long piece of driftwood as his drill in his left hand. He begins "drilling" pieces of wood, making a "Brrrrrrrrrrrrrrm" sound. He can visualize a piece of driftwood as a tool. This process of mentally representing objects will help Mariano learn the use of letter and number symbols when learning to read, write, and do math calculations.

Children experience math skills while constructing, including classifying, comparing, contrasting, seriating, and patterning. Charlie uses 4-by-4-inch redwood posts that have been cut in 4-, 8-, and 12-inch-long building blocks. As she makes a skyscraper with Diana and Drew, she classifies as she places all 12-inch blocks together, balancing each row of blocks atop the previous row to make a wall. She compares each new piece to the 12-inch pieces she is already using to determine if they are the same size. Charlie exhibits contrasting as she looks at Diana's wall to see how it is different from her wall. The builders work carefully, constructing strong walls that "will not fall down in the wind." Seriation or ordering is a higher level of comparing. It involves ordering items in a logical sequence according to a common attribute, such as size, volume, or weight. Diana displays an understanding of seriation as she arranges the redwood blocks by size. The girls connect their walls with an adjoining wall to make their skyscraper. Inside the enclosure, Drew is building an elevator. He illustrates patterning as he makes an elevator tower of alternating redwood blocks and wood planks. The children are developing other math concepts, such as symmetry, shape, size, number, space, geometry, fractions, and part/whole relationships.

4. Enhancing Physical Competencies

Work in the construction zone is physical and involves a lot of action and learning through movement. Large- and small-motor skills, eye-hand coordination, and visual perception are fostered as children decide how to construct with loose parts. Drew and Salvador lift, carry, balance, and transport wooden spools, railing support blocks, and arches to the carpet area for building on the patio. As they stack the pieces, they learn about how to maintain control of their body position (balance) while reaching high and standing on tiptoe. They gain an understanding of body awareness and how to negotiate stacking without knocking down the tower. Eye-hand coordination is used as Drew and Salvador control, guide, and direct their hands to place wood pieces in position. Each time their tower tumbles, the boys are quick to jump out of the way (sensory processing). The boys' ability to maintain attention and concentration to rebuild the tower is impressive. Since materials in the construction zone are open-ended, there are progressive physical challenges. Each child is free to continuously choose a level of challenge, thus building a personal progression.

5. Enhancing Expressive Arts

Building in the construction zone inspires children to think differently and create structures from imagination. Children are architects as they explore the art and science of designing buildings and structures. The elements of art shape children's creativity as they build. They use line, shape, form, color, space, and texture to create sculptures and architecture. Materials in the construction zone are made of wood, metal, and stone and are available in a variety of colors, textures, tones, shapes, and proportions. How children combine and place the materials determines a structure's visual appeal. Children experience proportion, symmetry, and the relationship between solid (walls, roof) and void (openings) as they build. Divergent thinking, the ability to solve a problem in multiple ways, is enhanced as children explore the science of building structures.

Drew and Sebastian work persistently to arrange boards into a tripod shape. They are challenged, as the boards do not remain balanced and continually fall. Repeatedly they persevere, trying out different sloping and orientation strategies for angling the boards against each other. After a lot of trial and error, the boards finally remain stable, creating a symmetrical pyramid. The boys squat down on opposite sides of the structure and peek at each other through open cracks in the planks. Success at last! As children move from discovery to more advanced stages of building, their ingenuity and creativity flourish in structures that include patterns, symmetry, and realistic representations. Their imaginations may take them to outer space, fantasy worlds, fire stations, or papa's house.

Essential Components: What Every Construction Zone Needs

Space: A building area attracts action, so it needs to be large enough to accommodate multiple children building large, complex structures. Strive for a 30-by-40-foot level space, although building often extends beyond the construction zone to other outdoor spaces. Having more than one building space accommodates different needs. A large open space with big loose parts allows for active building. An area with smaller materials works on an 8-by-10-foot rug. Some children prefer to build alone or with a friend in a more intimate space. If possible, locating a construction space under cover allows children to build on harsh weather days. There is nothing better to lift the spirits of both children and teachers than getting outside in fresh air.

Work space: Different levels in the space add interest and challenge to the large flat surface as well as allowing children to build high. Platforms, low tables, and mini sawhorses are good additions, as well as tree trunks, straw bales, tires, wood spools, flat boulders, and crates.

Ground surface: Concrete or asphalt are the best building surfaces, although play yard bark and gravel work. Children can stabilize pieces of 4-inch pipe by twisting them down into gravel or bark. Gravel is appropriate only for children over age three.

Construction zone before

Originally this space was a combined construction and large-motor area, which made it challenging for multiple children to build while other children engaged in large-motor activities. The ground surface was large rubber playground tiles to protect from falls. Large interlocking plastic building blocks offered building possibilities, but the interlocking design limited the balance, stability, and construction learning that standard unit blocks offer.

The large-motor zone was relocated to provide ample construction space for several builders. We wanted something more visually appealing than rubber tiles for the ground surface, but we had to shift our thinking when we discovered dirt under the tiles. Gravel became the most cost-effective option. For building materials, wooden blocks and black pipes cut into several uniform sizes are stored in crates and line the area's perimeter for easy access. We included gutters and wood planks for making inclines, along with sawhorses and wooden crates.

Top Tips for Designing Construction Zones

1. Provide a flat space large enough to accommodate multiple builders.
2. Cut building materials in several uniform sizes.
3. Keep a plentiful stock of materials so children can build large structures.
4. Organize and store materials in crates to keep them accessible.
5. Use crates and sawhorses to offer a variety of building levels that create interest and challenge.

Construction zone after

Enhancing construction zones: An investigative environment is key for children to experiment with balance, stability, gravity, and design. Rich, assorted building materials will inspire children to construct intriguing structures. The natural beauty of wood building materials makes the space aesthetically pleasing. Changes in the wood as pieces age create wonderful contrast. An abundance of building materials excites builders and invites them to build something big.

Construction Zone Tools and Materials

Typically, blocks are made from wood and purchased commercially. Building materials for an outdoor construction area, however, can be homemade from a wide variety of materials. Make your own block set with untreated redwood or cedar posts (4 inches by 4 inches by 8 feet) and black drainage pipe (4 inches by 10 feet). Cut long pieces into parts of 4, 8, and 12 inches. Just like unit blocks, it is important for pieces to have standardized sizes, shapes, and dimensions. The cut pieces need to be sanded to ensure smooth edges. Battery-powered sanders are fast and effective for adult use. Give children sanding blocks to smooth rough edges and sides. Sanding is a satisfying experience they will enjoy.

Planks in varied lengths (2, 3, and 4 feet) and widths (6 and 12 inches) may be handmade from redwood, western red cedar, and cypress. Check with your local lumberyard to determine the availability and cost of exterior lumber choices. Although not designed as an exterior wood, pine can hold up in protected areas and last for a few years even when fully exposed. Know that wood discolors over time to a rich, silvery gray color. Never use wood treated with chemical preservatives, such as is used on pallets.

Wood and plastic crates serve a double purpose in a construction area. They store material and are fabulous for creating large buildings. Wood crates are sturdy. Children can build structures they can walk on with wood crates and planks.

Bed risers are designed to lift furniture such as a bed frame off the ground. Although not designed as a children's play item, they work well as a loose part in a construction zone. They are heavy duty, are uniform in shape, can hold a lot of weight, and come in different heights.

Construction Pieces
Bed risers
Black corrugated pipe
Black PVC pipe (4 or 6 inches in diameter cut into 6-, 9-, and 12-inch pieces)
Cove molding (2- to 4-foot lengths)
Ladders (small)
Logs
Milk crates
Pallets
Planks (1 to 6 feet in length)
Pulley system
Redwood blocks (4-by-4-inch posts cut into 4-, 8-, and 12-inch lengths)
Sandbags (4 by 8 inches or 6 by 12 inches)
Sawhorses (mini)
Tires
Tree blocks
Tree trunks
Wood cables

Wood crates
Wood planks
Wood scraps

Loose Parts
Driftwood
Large rocks
Rope
Tin cans
Wood pieces

Bed risers offer intriguing building possibilities.

Homemade blocks in uniform sizes are made from untreated redwood posts.

Repurposed empty wire spools are a welcome addition to construction zones.

Storage and Organization

If possible, keep construction materials in the zone so that they are always ready and teachers do not have to haul them in and out each day. Crates work particularly well for storing construction materials. The slats allow ground surface materials in the zone, such as dirt, gravel, sand, and bark to fall through and not accumulate in the bottom. Line crates up along the perimeter of the space for easy access. Place similar items in the same crate. For example, all black pipe in one crate and wooden redwood blocks in another. Heavier crates or medium trash cans are needed to support the weight and size of long planks. Lighter crates may be used if planks can rest against the vertical surface of a building or fence, or children may find it easier to access planks propped against a wall or fence with no storage crate. Ski racks or coat racks with wooden dowels can be mounted on a fence so the planks rest between the dowels. Arrange crates of blocks on open shelves so that they are easily accessible. Smaller loose parts add interest and details to structures as well as extend and enhance play. These materials can be stored in containers or baskets.

Cleaning and Maintaining the Space

Cleaning up the construction zone is part of the daily routine. Children can help place materials in crates or stack them on shelves when there is a simple visual system. An organized zone makes it faster for builders to find materials and easier for them to put materials away. Sometimes children may request that their structures stay up so they may continue building. Unlike inside block areas, outside construction zones are not needed for other activities, so it may be possible to leave structures for an extended period.

Maintain the construction zone by gathering, adding, and replenishing natural loose parts to extend play, such as thick tree blocks and logs. Keep the construction zone safe by regularly checking for broken pieces and materials with rough edges. Sand items or replenish as needed. Replacing a few wood blocks, planks, or crates each year will eliminate the need for a major replacement all at once. Check pieces for mold or mildew, which may be an issue in damp climates. Catching mold early is key for successful eradication with a bleach solution. Store pieces in a dry, shaded area or under a covered work space if possible. A tarp can protect items during wet seasons. Excessive exposure to sun and precipitation are hard on wood.

The Extra Dimension

Tree blocks and tree cookies are a wonderful way to add rustic, natural materials to a construction zone. Collect fallen tree branches in different diameters from your yard, neighborhood, or nature hikes. Oak, cherry, walnut, camphor, aspen, poplar, ash, hickory, redwood, spruce, fir, cedar, and birch each provide distinct smells, colors, and textures. Be cautious with pine wood, as it can be very sappy. Green or fresh branches tend to split, revealing a V cut in the piece, so you may wish to let branches dry several weeks before cutting. Some people consider split pieces defective, although they are still usable. Cut branches with a handsaw or band saw. If using a handsaw, secure the branch in a vise to hold it firm while you cut. A band saw is fast and efficient. Be certain to follow all safety procedures when operating a band saw to avoid injury. Branches may be cut in different thicknesses and diameters. Leave the bark on pieces for texture. It may fall off with repeated use, but the tree block will still be good. Pieces cut in unusual shapes such as arches or Y's are particularly appealing. Since tree branches are natural, I always leave them natural. They may be rubbed with beeswax or coated with clear varnish for extra protection if desired. If you are not handy or do not own a saw, solicit help from school parents or family members to cut branches. One teacher asked her brother for tree cookies for her birthday. He was pleased to use his carpentry skills to create a free but meaningful gift, and she and the classroom children were thrilled with the tree cookies. Tree blocks are also available for purchase on the internet.

Supporting Equitable Learning

- Encourage both girls and boys to construct.
- Make construction zone surfaces and space accessible for wheelchairs and standing and walking aids.
- Plan for nonmobile children by offering block play on a tabletop or the ground.
- Help children find roles to play in the construction zone and facilitate adaptations and adjustments.
- Encourage more experienced builders to serve as experts to assist other children in their building challenges.
- Model building for children who speak different languages and for those who have diverse abilities.
- Provide different types of blocks for grasping.
- Add easy-to-manipulate lightweight blocks or blocks that attach to help children with less hand coordination.

Mini sawhorses offer support for building planks.

An outdoor rug serves as the construction zone for infants and toddlers in a family child care home.

When Drew discovered that wood planks could slide through the crate's slats, the structure transformed into a helicopter.

Infant/Toddler Construction Area Ideas

Stackable materials support the building efforts of infants. Here are some ideas:

- Large, smooth stones

- Plastic cups

- Smooth countertop tile samples. Residential samples are available for purchase on the internet and can sometimes be found at stores that sell upcycled materials.

- Tin cans (opened with a smooth-edge can opener)

- Tree blocks

- Wooden or metal bowls

Toddlers enjoy stacking, knocking over, balancing, and placing blocks. The key to supporting toddler builders is to store materials in the zone so that they are easily accessible. Building materials in a preschool construction zone are appropriate for toddlers, but one change to consider for toddler builders is offering shorter planks in 1-, 2-, and 3-foot lengths that are easier for them to manipulate. Provide low levels to build on: platforms, crates, and tree trunks. Toddlers like to transport as well as fill and dump. Offering buckets and baskets with handles, wagons, carts, or large dump trucks for children to move materials from one spot to another supports these interests.

Chapter 8
Trajectory Zones

Because the air quality index has been in the unhealthy zone, many days have passed since the children last played outdoors. Finally, in the late afternoon it is safe to go outside. In anticipation, teachers Lisa and Rosie set up a new trajectory apparatus for the toddlers. A large carpet tube and rain gutter are propped against the rungs of homemade wooden frames (resembling ladder ball frames). Who knew that a carpet tube could generate so much interest for Gavin, Liliana, Romi, and Wyatt? The four children run outside like lambs kicking up their heels in spring and rush over to investigate the new equipment. In a high, squeaky voice, Liliana says, "Up, down, up, down" as she pushes and pulls on the carpet tube's higher end in a seesaw motion. She moves to the tube's lower end and uses her strength to pull the tube up. The angled tube catches on the wooden rung above and stays put. Her focus shifts, and she places a ball in the rain gutter, stretching her arms out straight in front of her as the ball races down the incline. Meanwhile, Wyatt places a ball in the carpet tube. He peeks into the tube as the ball rotates down. He sends a second ball down the tube and watches intently as it goes swiftly down. He swings his arms, prances with delight, and then runs to join Gavin, who is collecting balls. Romi peeps through the tube's opening. She grasps the tube, places her face up to the opening for a couple of seconds, and then pulls her head away. She repeats the peeking motion several times, each time smiling broadly as she pulls away. Her fascination seems to be focused on hide-and-seek rather than rolling balls. She seems to think that she cannot be seen when her head is within the tube's opening. Gavin takes a turn at putting balls in the tube. He leans his body to the side and looks at where the ball exits at the far end rather than watching inside the tube. The foursome continue to experiment with trajectory for quite some time while simultaneously having fun finding and retrieving balls.

The Value of Trajectory Zones

Children have a fascination with movement. It captures and engages their interest for long periods of time. Their eyes fixate on moving objects, and their bodies enjoy the power and freedom of being the moving object themselves. This captivation is an action schema called trajectory. Horizontal trajectory is demonstrated when children kick balls, push dump trucks, and swing. Vertical trajectory is exhibited as infants repeatedly drop objects and watch them fall or young children squirt water from a hose up in the air. Diagonal trajectory is observed as children slide down a slide or roll a ball down an incline. Teachers are often quick to notice trajectory actions because some seem inappropriate, such as squirting someone else or knocking over another child's structure. Setting up specific spaces for children to explore trajectory can satisfy and redirect a child's trajectory urges to more appropriate experiences. Trajectory may be seen in multiple outdoor areas and in many ways. Spraying liquid watercolor with a spray bottle onto butcher paper in an art zone, pouring sand through a funnel in the sand area, or swinging are all trajectory experiences. Trajectory loose parts may be incorporated into construction, water, and sand zones. Simple machines such as catapults, pendulums, water pumps, and pulleys can be placed in different outdoor spaces. Or a designated space can be installed in the form of a trajectory wall that has ramps secured to a wall or fence.

Schema Learning

Transporting: moving and carrying tubes, pipes, rain gutters, and planks

Transforming: using construction materials to create ramps

Trajectory: rolling objects down planks, cove molding, gutters, pipes, and tubes; creating inclines; knocking down blocks; throwing objects; pushing wheelbarrows; climbing; sliding; swinging; jumping off equipment; squirting water on others; spraying with squirt bottles; pouring water or dumping sand; launching objects with a catapult; hoisting items with a pulley; swinging a pendulum; hammering; sawing; smashing things

Rotation: watching balls spin down chutes or thrown in the air

Connecting/disconnecting: creating inclines by attaching pipes or gutters; dismantling inclines

---

Trajectory Zones to Foster Learning

1. Enhancing Social and Emotional Competencies

As Ashton and Sammy work alongside each other at the trajectory wall, they learn about seeing things from another's point of view, sharing, helping, and taking and waiting turns. Ashton, who has more trajectory experience, provides help as Sammy struggles to place a ball in the top ramp. He provides less assistance as Sammy masters the task. This concept is known as scaffolding. Ashton and Sammy take turns leading and following as they alternate placing balls in the ramps. Later the two boys plan together as they stand on opposite ends of the trajectory wall and determine how and when to release balls simultaneously on different ramps.

Emotional competencies of perseverance, initiative, independence, and self-regulation are fostered as children spend long periods of time doing something that piques their curiosity and is intrinsically motivating. For Drew, this is experimenting with the speed and direction of balls racing down the chute. Each day he plays at the trajectory wall alone or with friends for a prolonged time. He practices self-control by waiting for balls to reach the ground and takes responsibility for not bumping into others who play alongside him. Drew tries sending multiple balls simultaneously down a chute with exhilaration rather than fear of failure. He can handle the stress when several balls are introduced on different tracks. Drew and other children release energy, test their theories, and control their actions during the captivating experience.

2. Enhancing Language and Communication Competencies

Trajectory spaces foster language and communication competencies as children formulate verbal directions for friends and translate others' directions into accurate action. Daisy directs others to place balls on ramps: "To the left, right, higher, lower, stop, go." She explains her actions to others: "If I start the ball here, it gets stuck, but when I put the ball up here, it goes fast all the way to the bottom." Communication and collaboration skills are gained as children work together to test their ideas. For instance, Sheila and Michael share their thoughts and negotiate as they build a "U-shaped" ramp structure with three rain gutters. They talk about how to place sandbags under gutters to make the right slope and to stop the balls at the end.

Becoming literate in physics and engineering concepts is like learning a new language. You need to have fun with the language and be willing to dive in, make mistakes, and watch others. As children repeatedly play with trajectory, they will feel increasingly comfortable and begin to understand it. Teachers can help children become literate by introducing language such as *rotate, direction, force, distance, collision, speed, time,* and *power*. Be sure to describe only what is seen and not why it is happening. Encouraging children to explain their theories, predictions, actions, and results fosters critical thinking and promotes inquiry. When adults explain what is happening, it limits children's thinking. Restate, clarify, or challenge their ideas rather than correcting them.

3. Enhancing Cognitive Competencies

Open-ended play with trajectory loose parts fosters children's cognitive competencies as they plan, test, problem solve, and investigate—all skills of scientific inquiry. This is seen as Kiley and Meredith position gutters of different lengths on a vertical board designed for trajectory. The girls explore how their arrangement changes the direction, angle, and speed of water flowing down. In his play, Cory develops his abilities in anticipation and prediction as he guesses which route a ball will take coming down the ramps. He practices visual tracking by watching the ball to confirm his prediction. Annalise is fascinated with the relationship between the degree of incline and the speed of balls rolling down planks. Each day she tries a new way to elevate the planks. She has tried a tree trunk, a crate, sandbags, and a mini sawhorse. Isaac too is captivated by slope and speed, using cove molding and Ping-Pong balls. He creates two tracks of equal distance and slope and varies one track by slipping a tunnel (cardboard tube) over it. He simultaneously releases balls and watches to see which lands first. Next, he lowers the slope of one track and notices that ball speed changes. Through his inquiry, Isaac develops temporal awareness by predicting and judging ball speed.

4. Enhancing Physical Competencies

Perceptual motor and motor development are core components to children's learning. Perceptual ability is how children perceive or take in their world, which includes themselves and everything that surrounds them. Children gather information through sight, touch, body sensations, hearing, timing, and other senses. Sensory information is organized and interpreted and then acted upon. The motor portion of perceptual motor abilities is the child's action or self-expression based on what has been perceived and interpreted.

Body control abilities, including kinesthetic awareness, balance (dynamic and static), reaction time, adaptability, and object manipulation, are fostered as children create ramps and explore movement. An understanding of body and space relationships develops as children experience the direction of ball movement. Spatial awareness improves as children arrange materials and position themselves while creating structures. Depth perception is strengthened as children determine distances for placing ramps. Children practice visual focus and visual tracking skills by watching balls roll down ramps. For example, Marybeth changes her focus as a ball changes direction or as more than one ball rolls.

Children gain strength and control over their bodies as they move wood planks, gutters, and pipes. For instance, Diana and Ari take hold of an 8-foot piece of perforated drainage pipe on opposite ends. It takes all their strength to drag the heavy pipe to the patio. Once the pipe is in place, the girls begin to rapidly fill the pipe on both ends with plastic balls. The balls disappear into the middle of the pipe. Each girl practices bimanual dexterity as she grasps the pipe in one hand while picking up balls with her other hand. The girls place the balls inside the pipe using eye-hand coordination.

5. Enhancing Expressive Arts

Expressive arts are visible in the three-dimensional designs of trajectory walls and ramp structures. Line, the most basic visual element of art, is prominent in trajectory compositions. Children see how lines have dimension: size, direction, length, width. Gutters mounted on a wall are horizontal, vertical, or diagonal (direction). Trajectory lines can be long or short (length), for instance, wood planks cut in 2-, 3-, 4-, and 6-foot lengths. The track of rubber base molding can be straight or curved or even wiggly. Lines can have weight, such as thick, heavy PVC pipe or skinny, light cove molding.

Essential Components: What Every Trajectory Zone Needs

Space: A rich assortment of materials that promote trajectory may be added to the construction, sand, and water zones. For example, buckets, shovels, and containers can be used for pouring sand. Gutter systems, funnels, water pumps, and clear tubing in a water area allow children to experiment with water flow. Tubes and ramps make inclines for balls and cars to roll down. Place simple machines such as pendulums and pulleys in different outdoor spaces. Pendulums move freely when suspended from a support such as rope. Swings are a great example. Pulleys can hoist items up to a platform or send tools in a bucket across the construction area. To make a pulley, tie a long rope to a bucket handle. Throw the rope up and over a sturdy tree branch. Secure the rope's loose end to something at ground level, such as the base of a tree.

Trajectory zone before

A trajectory zone did not previously exist in this family child care play yard. The area along the storage shed was unused play space.

The side of the storage shed became the perfect space for a trajectory wall. Pipe chutes were carefully placed on the shed wall, secured diagonally at appropriate heights so that children can reach. A tree trunk added on the left side can help a child reach. Pipe chutes are mounted with suitable inclines for balls to roll smoothly down them without stalling or falling off. Balls are stored in a container at the base of the trajectory wall.

Top Tips for Designing Trajectory Zones

1. Secure pipe chutes diagonally to a fence with suitable inclines, multiple drops, and appropriate heights.
2. Have a crate, step stool, or tree trunk available to stand on if additional height is needed.
3. Movable ramps such as tubes, pipe, and planks may also be added to allow children to control track design, construction, and experimentation.
4. Ramp stands provide elevation for creating slope.
5. Balls kept in containers are accessible and keep the space organized.

Trajectory zone after

Enhancing trajectory zones: Young engineers like to explore materials in spaces that are designed for tinkering. Think about items that can serve as ramps and bases, items to support bases, and items that roll or pour. Include loose parts that are not totally round, such as pine cones or napkin rings, as these objects will provide intrigue and opportunity to compare rotation and speed. Having a variety of ramp styles and balls offers children more opportunity to explore force and motion, compare, and learn about the properties of each object. Most ramps are rigid, and design work involves straight, flat lines. Ramps such as corrugated drainpipe and rubber base molding are flexible, however, allowing children to make loops, hills, and valleys with the track. Enhance trajectory spaces throughout the yard. Bamboo pipes and chutes make an exquisite trajectory wall as water flows through sluices. Add visual interest in water spaces with vibrantly colored water that rapidly flows down gutter inclines. Stones placed in gutters or a cascading water table glisten when wet and provide a beautiful natural element for water to run over. In the art area, spray art (colored water sprayed on paper) creates magnificent designs as water runs down the paper.

Trajectory Zone Tools and Materials

Inclines

Black corrugated
  drainage pipe
Black PVC tubes
Cardboard cove
  molding
Carpet tubes
Clear PVC tubes
Cove molding (1-,
  2-, 3-, and 4-foot
  lengths)
PVC pipe (4-, 8-, and
  12-inch pieces)
Rubber base molding
Sturdy cardboard
Vinyl rain gutters

White PVC tubes
Wood ramps

Bases to Support Inclines

Barrels
Boulders
Concrete blocks
Crates
Mini sandbags
Mini sawhorses
Pallets
Tree trunks
Wood frames with
  dowels
Wood frames with rope
Wooden spools

Things That Roll

Balls of all types (whiffle, handball, plastic
  baseball, ball pit,
  and wooden balls)
Canning rings
Hula hoops
Maple rings
Napkin rings
Pine cones
Spools
Stones
Tires
Tree cookies
Wheels

Things That Pour

Dirt
Gravel
Sand
Water

Wood frames with rope allow gutters to be propped at different inclines.

Storage and Organization

Trajectory materials need to be stored in the play zone where they are used. Crates work well for larger items, and galvanized or wire containers are useful for smaller items that roll. Select objects so they will fit into one container. Wall-mounted containers or buckets work well for trajectory wall storage. Secure containers to the vertical surface, hang a bucket over a picket fence, or place a container at the wall base.

Cleaning and Maintaining the Space

Trajectory spaces require limited maintenance, as materials such as drainpipes and rain gutters are designed for outdoors. Check vertically mounted chutes for stability, and secure as needed. Make certain there are no broken or sharp edges on loose gutters and pipes, and repair or replace pieces with damage. Trajectory balls seem to end up in odd places, so as you walk around the play yard, be on the lookout for loose balls. Balls may need to be replenished as the supply diminishes. Seek different weights, textures, and sizes of balls to add to the space.

The Extra Dimension

To create a trajectory wall with pipe chutes, purchase corrugated black drainage pipe (4 inches by 50 feet) at a hardware store. Use a band saw to cut the pipe in half lengthwise. If you do not have a band saw, solicit help from a parent, family member, or neighbor who does. You will now have two 50-foot trough pieces. Mount a long length of pipe diagonally on the

fence or wall. Make sure that children can place balls in the chute at the highest point, or place a crate on which shorter children can stand. Secure the top edge of the pipe about every foot with screws. If mounting pipe on chain-link fencing, make holes in the pipe's edge and use zip ties to secure the pipe to the fence. Add pieces of pipe above and below the foundation chute to create vertical drops. Pipe may be cut with pruning shears or heavy-duty scissors to get desired lengths. Balls should roll smoothly down chutes at a good clip without stalling or falling off. If inclines are too steep, balls will bounce off the chute. If there is not enough slope, balls will get stuck. The fun part is testing the chutes as you are placing them so they are arranged exactly right. It is helpful to have two people install pipe so that one person can hold the pipe in place while testing before permanently securing it. Adjust the pipe higher or lower depending on your research. Use your ingenuity to add multiple chutes so that balls may travel various directions and drop different ways. Trajectory walls may also be created with vinyl rain gutters. Use the same method as with drainage pipe to secure gutters to the vertical surface.

Supporting Equitable Learning

- Create simple, gentle slopes for children with less developed motor skills to roll objects down.
- Provide a variety of incline pieces, bases, and balls for children to grasp and maneuver.
- Provide a variety of loose parts options that engage children's senses.
- Provide varying heights of inclines to allow all children access.
- Stage trajectory options as inspiration for uncertain builders.
- Encourage both girls and boys to experiment.

Large holes cut in elbow pipes create additional openings for balls to be inserted at different levels and angles. This allows infants and toddlers to successfully place balls in the tube at their level and watch them roll.

Acrylic picture ledges angled from a wine rack allow water to flow down.

Rhys is captivated by trajectory of cascading water.

Heavy-duty magnets are attached to gutters of this homemade trajectory wall so that children can adjust slopes as desired.

Infant/Toddler Trajectory Zone Ideas

Infants track movement with their eyes and reach for objects to grasp. Not long after, they start to drop items and discover cause-and-effect relationships. Toddlers enjoy throwing objects and watching their trajectory. Here are some loose parts ideas to support infants' and toddlers' fascination with trajectory:

- Large buttons, canning rings, napkin rings, or wooden clothespins to insert into a wooden tissue box cover

- Metal or wooden rings to insert on a paper towel dowel and watch fall

- Felted balls to roll down clear or cardboard tubing

- Self-grip hair rollers, plastic pipe pieces, or balls to roll down an inclined sanded plank

- Sections of hardware chain to drop into a metal bucket

- Soft items to throw: squishy balls, hair donuts, soft-weave knotted balls, felted balls, bath loofahs

Chapter 9
Large-Motor Zones

Everett's large-muscle strength is impressive as he pulls himself up to stand while holding on to a large tree trunk for support. At 10 months, he can pull himself up with ease and no longer falls backward. He is strong enough to move around the trunk on uneven ground and bend down to grasp a piece of bark while standing. He explores the texture of the bark in his hand and then strikes the trunk with the bark. I wonder if he is attempting to make marks with the bark, as previously he spent focused time making marks with large hunks of chalk on slate. Greyson (age 12 months) gains confidence in navigating his environment as he climbs over a large piece of driftwood after Everett. Increased agility and motor-planning skills allow him to straddle the log, placing his hands and feet to stretch and steady himself. Both boys learned to pull themselves to a standing position by holding on to a log. Now they are testing and gaining confidence with their balance and strength. Certainly the boys' physical development is strengthened as they engage with these large-scale logs. The big natural objects afford different and unseen challenges and are the perfect large-motor area for infants and toddlers. No fixed equipment is needed.

The Value of Large-Motor Zones

A large-motor zone is a space for children to engage with tires, crates, long planks, and ladders in a wide variety of ways. Children use large-motor skills for arranging, stacking, rolling, climbing, constructing, balancing, hiding, and jumping. An outdoor play yard with movable items such as tires and planks makes a play space more exciting and flexible. Tires are one of the most multifaceted, economical, durable, and easily obtained loose parts. Children can construct, deconstruct, and reconstruct tires and planks daily into limitless configurations with increasing complexity and challenges. Tires and long wood planks are one of the best alternatives to children's climbing structures. Fixed playground equipment can be expensive to install and is designed for specific motor tasks such as climbing and sliding. Children tend to ignore structures over time once skills are mastered. Structures are permanent, unchanging, and unyielding to children's ideas. Large loose parts, including tires, crates, long planks, and ladders, are movable, versatile components that allow children to change and arrange their own environment.

Schema Learning

Transporting: carrying and moving wood planks, ladders, and crates

Transforming: using large loose parts to build obstacle courses and structures

Trajectory: rolling tires down a hill and jumping off planks, tires, and crates

Rotation: rolling tires and large wooden spools

Enclosing/enveloping: creating enclosed spaces with large loose parts; sitting inside a tire or crate

Connecting/disconnecting: making bridges and pathways to get from one side of an obstacle course to the other; taking materials apart

Large-Motor Zones to Foster Learning

1. Enhancing Social and Emotional Competencies

In a large-motor area, children play with large loose parts that foster independence, optimal risk, adventure, and creativity. This open-ended play is critical to growing resilient children. When children are free, trusted, and respected to figure things out on their own, they automatically learn how to work together. Socialization competency is promoted as children collaborate to build, alter, and enhance obstacle course challenges and negotiate differences with their playmates. Children learn how to lead and solve problems independently without needing an adult. One day Drew, Zachary, and Alexa work together to create a bridge from planks and tires. They roll and hoist tires, creating two levels. It takes united effort to navigate the four tires into place. Next, they position a plank between the tires to span the space. Alexa wants ramps on either end of the bridge for climbing on and off, but Zachary wants to jump off. The children compromise by having a ramp on just one end.

Children receive emotional satisfaction from mastering physical skills such as climbing up a plank or jumping off a crate. This joy is evident through their persistence to master a task through repeated trials and their delight after accomplishing it.

Teacher Cheri creates a bridge by placing a wide plank between two crates. On one end another plank is angled from the crate to the ground, extending above the crate. After crossing the bridge plank, two-year-old Mariano puts his foot onto the inclined plank. His weight elevates the plank into the air. He quickly removes his foot, causing the plank to drop, and then he steps cautiously with both feet onto the board. The board rises again and abruptly shifts downward as Mariano quickly descends the sloped ramp. He smiles when his feet touch the ground, and he hurries to repeat the motor task. Achieving such a risky action increases his self-confidence in his motor abilities. Attempting something that feels frightening or hard and persevering when something unexpected happens helps children develop resilience for overcoming future stressful situations.

2. Enhancing Language and Communication Competencies

Language and communication competencies expand in the large-motor area as children use descriptive words to express their actions and positions, have wants or needs fulfilled, exchange information, and gain social closeness. For example, Ari, Marlysa, and Alexa describe their actions and positions as they balance on a long plank positioned on top of three mini sawhorses. Ari says, "I got up this way [pointing to a plank propped against a wooden crate] to get away from the lava." Marlysa exclaims, "Watch me! Look, I'm on top of the world!" and "When I'm up here I can see over the fence!" For his part, Drew expresses his desire to have others chase him and Sebastian as they run on top of tires placed in a winding pattern on the ground. He shouts, "Come get us!" And Salvador states his need, "Hold that," as he hands a dinosaur to Bernadette before he bends down and crawls across a plank. As children climb up and down an obstacle course of inclined planks supported by mini sawhorses, they call out instructions: "Don't go down that way." Someone warns, "Look out, Drew! This board is wobbly."

Mariano, Zachary, and Ari gain social closeness as they talk with each other about their goal of building stacks of heavy car tires. Zachary rolls a tire closer, drags it next to the stack, and then shouts, "Hey, I need some help here" as he begins to hoist it up. Ari responds, "I'll help you. We can do it together."

Inclusive language and reciprocal conversation develop through play in the large-motor area.

Charley, Diana, and Alexa exhibit a high level of inclusiveness in their language while running around and jumping over pillows. Charley says, "Let's go," and begins to race in and out of eight pillows spread out in a long line on the ground. Next, Alexa encourages Diana and Charley to be frogs leaping over the pillows, saying, "We're frogs." The girls make a rib-biting sound as they gleefully jump over pillows. The three have reciprocal conversation as they move a long wood plank from the construction zone to the bark area. They listen to one another and respond appropriately ("We need to lift it higher," "Okay, I got it."). When two-year-old Bernadette approaches, Charley invites her to join in, saying, "You can help us." Later Charley describes how they "worked together" to carry the plank and create a bridge between two wooden crates. "We got the plank and made a bridge. We had a hard time carrying it. It was really heavy, but we did it."

Receptive language is demonstrated as Sebastian and Drew follow instructions for crossing an obstacle course, and Bernadette follows directions from Charley about where to grasp a plank. Drew uses expressive language to tell his friends how to do the obstacle course. "You go up here, then cross over. You can jump down here or keep going backward in this part. Going backward like me is hard." He demonstrates sequential language as he recalls the steps for completing the course and spatial language in his use of the words *up*, *over*, and *down*.

3. Enhancing Cognitive Competencies

Building climbing structures with planks, crates, and tires requires children to problem solve and understand cause and effect: estimating how far apart to place tires so that a plank may span the gap, finding ways to balance planks raised off the ground, and discovering different routes to get to the other side of an obstacle course. Children acquire knowledge through trial and error using their visual, auditory, tactile, and kinesthetic senses. A child cannot know that planks need to be secure to walk across them unless he has physically experienced stable and unstable surfaces. As Mark starts to climb a plank suspended between two tree trunks, the plank wobbles. He climbs off the tree trunk and adjusts the plank so that it is centered. Once in place, Mark climbs back up and crosses the plank. Later at group meeting time, the children view a video of their construction efforts. Mark's teacher asks him why he moved the plank. He looks at her and states matter-of-factly, "'Cause I was going to fall." His teacher challenges him about his reasons for moving the plank to elicit more of his thought process. Mark repeats that he was going to fall. Mark may not be able to articulate science concepts of gravity, force, stability, and balance, but he can perceive his surroundings and use past feedback and experience to steady a tottering plank. He can find solutions to challenges and understand cause-and-effect relationships.

On any given day, the large grassy area at Cheri's family child care is filled with children who are building with large parts. A collection of tires, wood crates, and wood planks puts the children in control of their own ideas. Children gain an understanding of measurement (length, width, and weight) as they carry and position long planks of wood and tires. They experience the concepts of vertical as they carry planks, horizontal as they prop planks across crates as balance beams, and diagonal as they place planks at a slant from tires to the grass. Zachary learns one-to-one correspondence as he jumps in and out of a line of tires placed on the ground. Early geometry concepts are visible as children apply their understanding of spatial relationships to building and navigating obstacle courses. Alexa and Diana are learning the spatial concept of position as they go in and out of the spaces of a ladder resting on its side, direction as they climb up a ramp, and distance as they navigate the obstacle course from near to far. The girls' knowledge of organization and pattern is further promoted as they arrange wood planks to fit across open spans.

4. Enhancing Physical Competencies

Children are naturally active, curious movers. The more they move, the more they learn about their bodies in space. Fundamental motor abilities of walking, jumping, climbing, and balancing develop through play in the large-motor area. Perceptual motor skills are seen when Sarah uses posture and balance to walk across planks and up and down inclined ramps. Walking across a wooden plank develops dynamic balance and improves visual motor skills. Dynamic balance is the ability to foresee and respond to changes in balance as your body moves in space. Structures built with tires, crates, and planks are more flexible than a fixed structure and require more advanced balance abilities. An understanding of directionality and laterality are enhanced as, for example, Thomas moves up, down, over, under, forward, and back on the obstacle course. Sammy walks clockwise around and around the rim of a tire. Jaxon walks up an incline board and jumps off the tire on which the board rests. Each day he challenges himself to jump off higher bases.

Muscle strength is needed to push, pull, move, and position heavy tires. Rolling tires up and down hills is a physical challenge. For instance, Zachary discovers that it takes even greater strength to roll a tire uphill than on flat ground. Children create a bridge by propping a wide plank between a mini sawhorse and a tree stump. Salvador challenges himself by placing his foot on the sawhorse rung, pulling himself onto the plank, and crawling along the board. In another space, Alexa challenges herself by climbing up a ramp that rests against two stacked tires. She walks across a plank and jumps off two stacked tires at the other end. She smiles proudly after landing in the grass. Salvador and Alexa are each gaining a sense of spatial awareness as they change their body positions to maneuver the obstacle course. Short ladders added to the large-motor area require more advanced physical control. Nicholas pretends to be a dog and walks with his hands and feet on the rungs of a horizontal ladder laid on the ground.

5. Enhancing Expressing Arts

The large space, unlimited time, and access to large, open-ended materials invite children to engage in creative play. For example, Mariano makes a "vrooooom" sound as he straddles a tire wedged vertically inside a second tire laying horizontally on the ground. He is riding his motorcycle. On other days, he has pretended to gallop his horse and drive his race car on this simple tire structure. Loose parts in the large-motor space at teacher Cheri's program have become a castle, house, and spaceship. A beloved tree in the space died and was cut down, but the remaining stump has become part of the children's imaginative play: a platform from which superheroes leap and a nest for children pretending to be hawks. Charlie and Alexa resourcefully stretch the plank across crates to create a bridge for reenacting "The Three Billy Goats Gruff." Later tires and planks turn into a pirate ship.

Essential Components: What Every Large-Motor Zone Needs

Space: Expansive space is necessary, as children will be building obstacle courses and large-scale structures. Grass or play yard bark are good ground surfaces for the area. Locating the area next to a fence or building has storage benefits, as tires and planks can be propped up against the vertical surface.

The large-motor area consisted of a gray plastic climbing castle, one tire, a canoe with a few large balls, and wooden trunks carved into stools. Children's activity in the space tended toward running with no sustained periods of engagement.

Large-motor area before

Large-motor area after

The existing space was large enough for building obstacle courses and had bark, a good ground cover. We replaced the climbing castle and canoe with large, open-ended materials that provide more risk and engagement. Tires, wood planks, a mini trampoline, and large logs were added to the stump stools.

Enhancing large-motor zones: Rather than designing a large-motor area around a climbing structure, enrich the space with tires and planks as the heart of the area. These large loose parts are unexpected and offer a physically stimulating, flexible, and challenging environment. Each day children may combine the loose parts in familiar or exciting new ways. Access to these materials affords children multiple opportunities to encounter challenges and reasonable risks. Make the area more aesthetically pleasing by adding large tree trunks from different types of trees. Redwood, eucalyptus, oak, and palm tree trunks provide varying color and texture.

Large-Motor Zone Materials

Tires: Recycled tires in a variety of sizes are available for free at any tire repair and service shop. Consider passenger tires for younger children and light truck tires for older children who need more of a physical challenge. Be certain to closely examine tires to ensure that there are no exposed steel belts offering a protrusion or laceration hazard. Clean tires thoroughly by scrubbing them with dish soap and a heavy scrub brush to remove grease and road oil from the wheel surface. Then rinse them before allowing children to play with them. Reusing tires for play not only helps to curb their negative impact on overcrowded landfill space, but it also teaches children about upcycling discarded objects for a new use.

Planks: Solid wood planks that are 11 inches wide and 6 to 8 feet in length allow children to build balance beams, bridges, and large obstacle courses. They are strong enough to stand on and walk across. Narrower boards (3½ to 4 inches wide) add a balancing challenge.

Barrels

Benches

Boulders

Corrugated drainpipe (4 inches wide)

Logs

Milk crates

Mini ladders

Mini sawhorses

Pallets

Planks or walking boards (narrow planks: 6 inches by 8 to 10 feet; and wide planks: 1 foot by 6 to 8 feet)

Platforms or sturdy wooden boxes for jumping

Solid wood crates

Tires (car and truck)

Tree trunks

Wood cable spools

Tires may be obtained for free from a tire store.

Corrugated drainpipe (4 inches by 50 feet) can be purchased from a hardware store and cut to desired lengths. It is lightweight, flexible, and durable, which makes it a highly effective loose part for the large-motor area.

Storage and Organization

Storing materials in the large-motor area is a matter of organization and access. Arrange materials along the perimeter so children can get and return them independently. Balance long planks against a fence or wall. Prop tires upright against a vertical surface that is protected from water. Remember that children like to transport, so carrying large materials to a large-motor area is a fun challenge. Materials left on grass will kill it, so store items off of grass when not in use.

Cleaning and Maintaining the Space

Take care that tires do not collect water, debris, or insects. Improperly stored tires can become breeding grounds for mosquitoes, which carry disease, so the tire liner must stay dry. Remove tires at the end of the day to a dry area away from sprinkler systems. During wet seasons, store tires in a vertical position and cover securely with a tarp. Do not lay covered tires horizontally, as water will pool in the tire's center and weigh down the tarp. It takes less effort to cover tires with a tarp than to remove accumulated water. Drainage holes may be drilled into tires, although I find this hard to do and unnecessary if tires are stored properly. Educators who have tires in their outdoor environments report that spiders and other insects rarely take up residence in tires that are used regularly. If tires have not been used for a while or you are concerned, swipe the inner liner of the tire with a cobweb brush before use. Wood planks need to be checked periodically for splinters and visible signs of splitting. Consider replacing one or two boards a year as part of regular maintenance. Planks will last outdoors without any protection for several years, depending on weather conditions.

Health Concerns and Reused Tires

I am commonly asked whether adding tires to play yards is safe. Hazardous chemicals are involved in the manufacture and composition of tires, so it is logical to be concerned that small amounts of harmful chemicals may be emitted from tire rubber over time through frequent contact with children's hands or in hot weather. Research exists about the impact tires have in landfills as well as recycled tire crumb rubber used as infill for playing fields. A report released in 2019 by the US Environmental Protection Agency (EPA) on tire crumb rubber characterization research activities stated, "In general, the findings from the report support the premise that while chemicals are present as expected in the tire crumb rubber, human exposure appears to be limited based on what is released into air or simulated biological fluids" (2019). But my position is that shredded rubber should not be in places where children will encounter it. Tires discarded in a landfill and shredded tire products are quite a different situation, however, than tires used in a play yard. I have heard a lot of stories about the dangers of tires with children, although the information seems to be based on hearsay or widely circulated narratives and not solid research. The US Consumer Product Safety Commission's *Public Playground Safety Handbook* identifies automobile tires as appropriate equipment for playgrounds, stating that tires require more advanced balance abilities than rigid climbers (2015). My advice is for you to conduct your own research and determine whether tires are an appropriate play option for your program.

Safety, Hazards, and Risk

Accidents occur when young children get in over their heads on fixed equipment or attempt to imitate the activities of more skilled children but do not yet have the capabilities. Additionally, when children's skills exceed the challenges provided by fixed equipment, they will try risky play, such as standing up in a swing, jumping off a swing, or climbing on the outside of a tube slide (Sawyers 1994). A favorable safety option to fixed equipment is loose parts. Children increase their personal risk level gradually when they are in control of designing and changing loose parts such as tires, planks, and spools, which offer diversity, flexibility, novelty, and adaptability.

Hazards are potential sources of harm. They are objects that children cannot see or be expected to avoid (Almon 2013). It is the responsibility of educators to protect children from hazards. Educators can reduce hazards in the large-motor area by doing these things:

- Checking the area regularly for hazards and removing them. For example, an exposed tree root in the middle of the play zone is unexpected and could become a tripping hazard. Dangerous items such as broken glass could cut a child.

- Implementing a maintenance schedule to replace worn loose parts.

- Providing careful supervision of children's play.

Risk is thrilling and exciting. It involves uncertainty and the possibility of an unintentional injury. According to Sandseter (2007), most outdoor risky play falls into six categories: play with great heights, play with high speed, play with harmful tools, play near dangerous elements such as fire or a steep cliff, rough-and-tumble play, and play where children disappear or get lost. Risk varies according to circumstances and our personal values, experiences, and comfort. Perceived risk and actual risk are not always the same. As you supervise children's play, assess whether the play is extremely risky or reasonably risky. Remember that risk is a natural part of life and beneficial to children's development. Educators can promote healthy risk in the large-motor area by taking these measures:

- Providing unstructured, sturdy play materials (loose parts) that can be freely manipulated.

- Trusting children to recognize and evaluate challenges and decide on a course of action that is not dangerous. Monitor play closely to determine when intervention is necessary.

- Fostering opportunities for risk-taking.

- Allowing children to master increasingly challenging play.

- Not placing children on equipment. If children cannot do it themselves, they are not ready for the challenge.

- Not providing loose parts that are wet, slippery, or uncomfortably hot.

Risk management can be complicated, but being proactive helps prevent injuries. Play yard risk-benefit assessments available on the internet and through insurance companies can help you ensure a healthy balance between safety, risk, and challenge.

The Extra Dimension

Mini ladders add an element of risk and challenge to a large-motor area. Climbing a ladder propped against a tire provides a different motor experience than climbing a solid board. Walking across a ladder stretched between two tires or crates requires balance and visual motor skills. Two-, three-, or four-rung ladders that are 36 to 48 inches tall and 16 inches wide may be made with wood from any lumberyard. Space rungs 15 inches apart. Printable templates for constructing a ladder may be found on the internet.

Supporting Equitable Learning

Allow children to use equipment independently (get on and off tires and planks). Do not assist them in using equipment beyond their skill level.

Emphasize quality of movement rather than speed.

Modify obstacles as needed. For example, adjust planks to lessen an incline or shorten a distance.

Allow time for children to continually redesign and alter loose parts to increase their levels of risk slowly and incrementally.

Encourage children who have different skill levels to help each other, and encourage all children to actively participate.

Teacher Aubrey's dad always brings great finds to the center. One of his best finds was truck tires.

This large dirt hill can be scaled in multiple ways.

A small-scale ramp structure was built for infants to climb up.

Large loose parts afford opportunity for children to construct challenging obstacle courses each day.

Infant/Toddler Large-Motor Zone Ideas

Set up a large blanket on top of a canvas tarp outdoors and place large loose parts slightly beyond infants' reach to stimulate crawling and experimentation. Consider adding napkin rings, wooden bowls, silicone trivet rings, or dog pull ropes. Infants can crawl over and around pillows of varying sizes. Large pieces of smooth wood are perfect for infants to master pulling themselves up to stand. Another way to invite standing is to place a sturdy crate underneath the blanket.

Chapter 10
Sand Zones

Maverik (age three) climbs over the wood border into the elevated sand area. He spends a lot of time in the sandpit mixing sand and water. Teacher Aubrey pulls over the garden hose, hands the end to Maverik, then turns on the water. A slow stream of water starts to flow out of the hose. Maverik quickly places the nozzle end into a T-shaped pipe fitting attached to the top of a vertical pipe buried in the sand. The fitting's purpose is demonstrated as Maverik puts water into the top of the hollow pipe and water flows out the fitting's end. His task is to secure the hose so that his hands are free to dig. After persevering for a few minutes without success, he pushes the hose deep enough into the pipe to stabilize it. The water begins to pool at the base of the pipe. Maverik picks up a sturdy shovel and begins digging. He grasps the shovel's handle with both hands down low, close to the blade. He holds on tight and puts the shovel's blade in dry sand at the water's edge, taking out a wedge of dry sand. Again, he puts pressure on the shovel with his arm strength as he plunges the blade. But this time he drives into heavier wet sand. He continues to dig and piles sand off to the side. The work is long and hard, but he works tirelessly on his own. His protruded

tongue is evidence of his high level of concentration and exertion as he tries to accomplish a challenging task. He digs a trench starting at the pipe stretching across the width of the sandpit, directing water away from the pipe. Does Maverik have a goal in mind, or is it the process of digging itself that is captivating to him? It seems as if he wants to direct the water's movement rather than stop it. Through play in the sand area, he has learned he can master problems. He has confidence that he can figure things out.

Schema Learning
Transporting: carrying containers and buckets; pushing dump trucks
Transforming: mixing water and sand or water and dirt
Trajectory: dumping sand
Rotation: stirring sand and water
Enveloping: burying items in the sand
Disconnecting: smashing sandcastles

The Value of Sand Zones

There is nothing quite like the marvelous sensorial and tactile qualities of sand. Whether it is fine, dry desert sand; wet, moldable play yard sand; or coarse riverbed sand, the material and its changeability are magnetic to children. It is critical for children to have an environment that supports play with the natural elements of sand, dirt, and water. A sand area is space for children to dig, tunnel, trench, excavate, dump, and make sandcastles and mud pies. Infants explore the properties of sand by grasping, releasing, patting, smoothing, and tasting it. They watch as it runs through their fingers to the ground and kick their feet to uncover their toes. Filling and dumping are a favorite activity for toddlers as well as transporting. Duncan fills a dump truck with sand, pushes it over to a mound, and dumps it. Preschoolers become more skillful at using tools and executing their ideas. Geoff and Caitlin build roads while Sherri makes cupcakes in a muffin tin. Destroying sand constructions is just as satisfying or perhaps even more so as building them. Sand is an ideal medium for children's inquisitive, physical, and imaginative nature.

Sand Zones to Foster Learning

1. Enhancing Social and Emotional Competencies

Children engage in an active social scene, with planning, compromising, negotiating, and sharing, as they work together to build dams and rivers, construct roadways, dig trenches, and create sandcastles. Plans are discussed. Compromise happens as children decide to build dinosaur land rather than roads. They negotiate roles to decide who will build a volcano and who will make a moat. Sharing and more negotiation take place as children decide how to take turns squirting the sand with water from the garden hose. Children collaborate as they engage in functional play by using shovels to fill up a bucket; constructive play by building walls, tunnels, and ditches; and dramatic play by creating and pretending to eat sand pies, muffins, and cakes. On one day, Humberto, Jorge, and Eduardo use large metal ice scoops to dig a deep hole in the sand and then wedge a galvanized tub into the space. They mostly work in silence as they fill the tub with sand. Jorge uses a large river rock to compact the sand while Eduardo uses his shovel. Every now and again a few words are said, but for the most part the boys' focus is on accomplishing their task. Surrounded by a beautiful natural landscape of tall grasses, tree trunks, and river rock, Clarice and Kelci sit on a log that borders the sand area to slip off their sandals and laugh as they bury their feet in the warm sand. Clarice squeals, "A river!" as water from a garden hose spreads out into a wide, shallow stream. The two girls venture into the stream and begin digging, filling buckets, and dumping wet, saturated sand. They are joined by Will and Cruz, and together they work tirelessly to shovel out a pond. Clarice grabs a long wood plank and with Will's help lays it over the water hole. The children take turns walking slowly across the plank, careful not to fall into the alligator pond below. As the hot summer morning and sensory play progresses, the alligators travel on. The children's interest shifts to piling sand high. Each shovelful of sand is thrown on the growing mound and patted down with the backs of shovels. They are making a humungous birthday cake. Kelci excitedly declares, "This is the best day ever!"

Playing with natural elements like sand can benefit a child's emotional welfare. Through purposeful, self-directed play, children gain independence, initiative, confidence, and a sense of achievement. Working with sand is very satisfying, as there is no right or wrong way to use it, and there is always an element of surprise and excitement. Children can express their emotions while playing without having to verbalize their thoughts. Heavy work, sensory input that engages the proprioception sensory system, is one of the best ways for children to regulate behavior and release energy and emotions. In the sand area there are many opportunities for heavy work: digging, hauling, pushing, and pulling heavy loads of sand in buckets, wheelbarrows, and dump trucks. Everett is action driven. The sand area affords him lots of space and loose parts to engage his body through movement. Today his focus is leveling a huge mound of sand. He uses tremendous force as he pulls and pushes sand with a rake. T. J. grabs a rake and silently starts to work alongside Everett, and together they flatten the sand mound.

2. Enhancing Language and Communication Competencies

Digging holes, filling buckets, and making mud pies can be social activities that require listening and speaking. Children develop descriptive language to express sand qualities (*gritty, fine, wet, smooth, coarse, loose, sticky, lumpy*) and sand play (*sieve, funnel, trowel, sift, scoop, pour, drag, flatten*). Children use comparative language to talk about similarities and differences in size, shape, and function of sand tools, as when Aaron describes how heavy his bucket is and explains he needs more sand because he is building a long road. On the far side of the sand area, Yu Yan scoops sand with a large spoon and watches its trajectory as she pours it into a pot. "It's full!" she announces, showing an understanding of the concept of full and empty.

Children provide directions to others or talk about their actions using spatial language. For instance, Micah is absorbed in making donuts. He tells Henry to put the bowl of batter next to the tray. He uses an ice cream scoop to place mounds of wet sand on the tray and then pours a fistful of sand on top. He explains how "You sprinkle sugar [sand] on top of donuts before putting them in the fryer to cook for 10." Lots of conversation takes place as children engage in dramatic play scenarios and reenact roles.

Children communicate their actions and the actions of others during sand play. After experimenting for quite some time making sandcastles, Rosemary seems to have perfected her technique. She carefully fills a metal plant pot with wet sand, pats it down, and quickly turns it over. She gives a solid thump to the bottom of the pot with her fist before lifting it up. A perfect sandcastle is revealed. "How did you do that?" Marissa asks. Rosemary responds, "Here's how," and uses a sequencing narrative to retell her steps. She is quick to clarify that "sand needs to be just right; not too dry or too wet 'cuz it won't work." She exaggerates the thump on the bottom of the pot and ends with "Ta da!"

3. Enhancing Cognitive Competencies

While playing in the sand, children gain an understanding of its physical properties by exploring and comparing dry and wet sand. For example, Misha discovers that dry sand flows freely as he lets it run through his fingers. However, when he wets his hand in a bucket of water and touches sand, the dry sand sticks to his wet hand. He shakes his hand and then rubs it on his shirt to get the sand off. He pours water on sand and notices that the sand is now moldable. He shapes the wet sand into small and tall mounds. He problem solves to keep taller sand mounds from collapsing.

Introducing ramps, gutters, funnels, sieves, orange cones, and tubes in a sand area allows children to explore movement and engineering concepts. For instance, Megan and J. D. stabilize a gutter against a large boulder in the sand area. They pour dry sand into the gutter and watch it flow down the incline. J. D. pulls over an outdoor funnel stand that holds three funnels of varying sizes and positions it over the gutter. He pours sand into the largest funnel and observes as sand falls to the gutter's side and piles on the ground. He adjusts the stand slightly so that sand cascades into the gutter. The children add a second gutter parallel to the first one and experiment with different sizes of funnels. A pulley system to move buckets of sand across the sand area or up to a platform allows children to try out a simple machine and reinforces STEM (science, technology, engineering, and math) skills.

Children are natural scientists in the sand area as they use the same skills that underlie scientific reasoning: noticing, questioning, predicting, experimenting, and discussing results. This inquiry process is evident as Benjamin explores impressions in the sand. Benjamin notices that he can leave a handprint in dry sand, although the imprint is not clear. He wonders how to make a more noticeable one. He explores wet and dry sand and discovers he can see his handprint more clearly in wet sand. His research leads him to conclude that wet sand holds hand impressions better. He extends his play by adding more water to the wet sand. He makes a handprint in the mushy mixture and is surprised to see that his hand impression disappears quickly. Benjamin makes a handprint in the medium-wet sand as if to test his previous finding. He smiles as a well-defined imprint is seen. Differences in his experience necessitated a return to his investigation and new explorations.

Mathematical concepts including comparison, shape, spatial sense, and measurement advance during natural experiences with sand. Children build roads in the sand that are wide or narrow, long or short. Loads of sand may be heavy or light, and a bucket may be empty or full.

Various containers allow children to explore the properties of three-dimensional shapes: cylinders, cubes, and rectangular prisms. Children apply spatial relationships to construction projects in the sand. For example, as Jaxon digs a trench in the sand, Lincoln navigates a wheelbarrow around a tire and alongside Jaxon's trench. This work increases their understanding of how to position and move objects and their bodies in the sand area. Beginning measurement concepts of volume, weight, and temperature are learned through trial and error as children play with dry and wet sand. When Ruby scoops sand into a bowl or pot, she strengthens her understanding of volume. Serenity discovers that wet sand weighs more than dry sand, and more sand is heavier than less sand. Quinn encounters temperature as she puts her bare feet into the sand. The top layer of sand is warm, but just a few inches down, the sand is much cooler.

4. Enhancing Physical Competencies

Sand play extends large- and fine-motor skills, spatial awareness, and body awareness. The weight of sand strengthens large muscles as children push, pull, transport, pour, shovel, and dig. Being barefoot in the sand increases foot and leg strength, agility, balance, and coordination as children adjust to the unstable surface.

Fine motor skills develop as children manipulate sand tools to sift, scoop, and stir. Daniela squats down in the sand area to investigate a flat piece of driftwood, then uses it as a spoon to scoop up sand and empty it into a bucket. Later she compares tools as she uses a real serving spoon to scoop sand. She adjusts her grasp to the spoon's handle. Through this sensory play, Daniela is using small motor skills and identifying items by touch. She is discovering the properties of sand, how it feels, and how it responds to her actions.

Children demonstrate spatial awareness as they gain greater motor control and navigating skills, such as scooping sand into a funnel, searching for a buried rock, or respecting another child's space. An understanding of body awareness expands as children kneel or squat in the sand and bend, twist, turn, rotate, and stretch.

5. Enhancing Expressive Arts

As children have repeated experiences with sand, their imaginations and creativity flourish. The transient nature of sand allows children to try out ideas, destroy creations, and begin again. The focus is on the process of creating rather than making a product. Sand as visual art includes drawing, sculpting, designing, and imaginative play. Children draw in sand with fingers, sticks, notched floor trowels, brushes, and combs. The temporary drawings are erased with a hand stroke or washed away with water. Children make sculptures by filling a container with damp sand, placing it upside down, and removing the container. Using containers of varying shapes and sizes as well as hand sculpting creates unique sculptures that are abstract or realistic. Children adorn sand creations with beautiful designs, using natural materials. For instance, Emersyn and Reese use sticks, acorns, eucalyptus pods, leaves, and seashells to decorate their sand cakes, pies, and cupcakes. Today they cover a mound of sand with small seashells and line up stones around its base. One single stick inserted into the top of the mound becomes a candle. It is a birthday cake for Reese's baby brother Luke, who is turning one year old. A lot of imaginative play in the sand area revolves around cooking as children imitate family members making familiar foods. For many children, sand play is safe and soothing, so they can freely use their imaginations to be anything they desire. Luis sprawls out on his tummy in the sand. He uses his hands as shovels in a swimming motion to dig a hole, sand flying. He looks up, supports his weight on his elbows, and says, "Me gopher." Evidently, he is reenacting the gophers who have been digging holes in the play yard grass.

Essential Components: What Every Sand Zone Needs

Space: When considering where to locate the sand area, look for an out-of-the-way space that has access to sun, shade, and water. Placing the sand area in a back corner along a fence perimeter works well. A back corner provides protection from more vigorous activities, such as swinging, climbing, and bike riding. Most sand will fall off shoes and clothing as children make their way to the classroom if the sand area is across the yard.

The ideal location for a sand area is partially in the sun and partially in the shade. Sun provides warmth in the winter, and sunlight helps keep sand bacteria-free. Shade is necessary for hot days in the summer. Umbrellas or sail or shade cloth anchored to a fence or building and stretched above the area are good options. Trees can be helpful providers of shade; however, leaves dropped in sand get messy.

A water source nearby is desirable. Dry sand play is exciting, but water adds many more possibilities. An outdoor faucet nearby allows children to use a hose and control their water needs. Another solution is to provide water in gallon jugs with spigots for children to access independently. While water added to sand enriches exploration, it is important for children to understand that water is a precious resource that needs to be respected and conserved. As educators, we have a responsibility to help children grasp water-saving concepts and teach them why we must not waste water. Involve children in deciding how to conserve water. Encourage them to suggest ways to reduce water use in the sand area and to be advocates for conserving water. Install a rain harvesting system in the play yard for children to monitor and learn that water is limited and dependent on seasonal rainfall. Add a hand-operated water pump attached to a tub. Fill the tub with the desired amount of water at the beginning of the day. Children will need to be careful to make the water last.

Size: Sand areas need to be exceptionally large to accommodate the active, heavy play of multiple children. Smaller, more protected spaces can be designed for infants and toddlers. A guide is 16 square feet per child under age three and 36 square feet per older child. An area at least 25 feet by 25 feet is a good amount of space for larger numbers of children, although even more square footage is recommended. Try to double the size that you think you need, as most people really underestimate it.

Depth: Sand needs to be a minimum of 20 inches deep so children can dig holes, trenches, and tunnels.

Building the area: Rake the area to remove clumps of dirt and rocks, and then level the space as desired. If drainage is an issue, consider placing a layer of gravel 5 to 10 inches thick as the bottom surface. Lay heavy-duty weed matting over a gravel or ground surface to prevent plant growth.

Borders: Sand areas need well-defined borders to contain the sand. Natural borders bring warmth, beauty, and texture, and intriguing spaces can be custom designed with boulders, river rock, tree trunks, and logs. Start with a plan but allow the setting and natural components to guide you. For example, the size and shape of tree trunks will dictate placement and dimensions of the area. The best designs often unfold and morph during their construction. Tree trunks and logs also provide good sitting spaces. Consider how children will access the area. Low borders such as river rock or large round wood slices allow easier access for younger children, but they may allow the sand to migrate to adjacent areas. A bridge into the space is a welcome transition.

Type: Types of sand vary in color, texture, and composition. Select only natural river, beach, or play yard sand that is recommended for children's play yards. Bags of play sand available at big-box stores have the advantage of being pre-washed, screened, and allergen free. However, it is usually more cost efficient to purchase play sand in bulk from a landscape supplier. Avoid builder's sand, as it is coarse and has added chemicals to help it mix with cement.

Sand zone before

The small sand area at this center was defined by a plastic border and tucked away in the corner of the yard. The space accommodated just a few children at a time.

Sand zone after

The sand area was expanded along the back fence from the hedge on the far left to the concrete patio on the right. The new dimensions are 18 feet by 12 feet, which now accommodates multiple diggers. A bridge serves as a passage that leads children into the space. Tree trunks of varying heights border the area for a natural look and contain the sand. River rock along the front adds to the natural aesthetics. Plastic sand tools were replaced with metal buckets and natural shovels of abalone, scallop, and coconut shells.

Top Tips for Designing Sand Zones

1. Border the area with tree trunks and river rock for a natural look and to contain the sand.
2. Ensure the area is large enough for active play of several children.
3. Ensure the sand is deep enough for children to dig and tunnel.
4. Provide metal buckets, spades, and natural shovels, such as abalone, scallop, and coconut shells.
5. Use open-frame baskets to provide organization and visibility and to allow sand to fall through.
6. Add an accessible transition into the space, such as a bridge.

Enhancing sand zones: Sand in sensory tables, tires, or large planter boxes provides different play possibilities in an outdoor area. Such spaces allow children to stand or kneel while engaged in sensory exploration. The disadvantage is that children do not have the option of large, active sand play. A wonderful material option for a sand table is small beach pebbles. Mexican beach pebbles have been naturally smoothed by ocean waves. The colors range from light gray and buff to moss green, charcoal, and rust. They make a magnificent sound as they are poured and scooped with metal containers.

Sand Zone Tools and Materials

Having a variety of open-ended materials in the sand area will affect the kind of play that occurs. Consider materials to support children's interest in digging, pouring, trajectory, transforming, constructing, pretending, and cooking. Adding fascinating accessories will provide new discoveries, challenges, engagement, and joy.

Digging Tools	*Natural Resources*	*Containers and Construction Tools*
Kitchen utensils	Abalone shells	Funnels
Scoops (metal)	Bark	Gutters
Shovels	Coconut shells	Metal buckets—various sizes
Spades	Large rocks	Muffin tins
Spoons (metal)	Scallop shells	Pie pans
Sticks	Seashells	Pipes
Trucks, diggers, bulldozers	Stones (small and large)	Ramps
	Tree trunks	Sheets of heavy plastic for building lakes, rivers, and dams
	Wood	Sieves
		Tin cans
		Tubes

Wood curio frames are upcycled into sand molds.

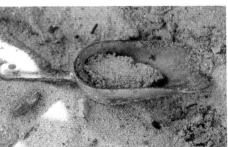

Replace plastic shovels with coconut, abalone, and scallop shells.

Storage and Organization

Having a limited amount of equipment is better than having too much. Too many items add visual clutter and restrict children's play. Materials that are not in use should not be left in the sand, but keeping materials outside all the time saves time and effort. Open shelves along the perimeter allow children to see what is available and independently access and return materials. Heavy crates or trash cans work well for holding spades, planks, gutters, and tubes. Hang spades, shovels, and buckets that have handles on hooks secured to a fence or building. Crates with slats or other small open-framed containers can hold kitchen-type utensils as they are easy to transport and sand slips right through, but avoid deep crates, as children must rummage through them or dump them out.

Open-frame wire baskets are used to see materials and for sand to fall through.

Cleaning and Maintaining the Space

The sand area must be covered at the end of each day to protect it from neighboring cats and other animals. Mesh covers allow for natural cleansing and aeration. Great options for a cover are insect screen or shade cloth, as both materials allow water and sunlight to permeate but prevent leaves and other debris from getting into the sand. Either material is a durable, lightweight mesh fabric that may be purchased in rolls of various widths and lengths, cut to fit, and attached to a PVC pipe for a simple roll-up cover. It can be rolled up in the morning and rolled back out at the day's end with little effort.

Another good cover option is using vinyl lattice sheets, found in the garden section of a hardware store. Lattice may be cut to the exact size and shape of the area. For irregular sand areas, place lattice on top of the sand. Draw out border lines on the lattice with a permanent marker and then cut the shape with a saw. Label the top and bottom or left and right for easy placement. Lattice pieces may be hung on a fence or moved out of the way while the sand area is in use.

Tarps are not the best cover option for sand areas. Rain or sprinkler water pools on top, making it a challenge to take off. Additionally, puddles of water attract mosquitoes, and wet sand under a tarp can harbor bacteria. If using a solid tarp, make sure to let the sand dry thoroughly before covering it for the night.

Any cover must be well fitted and secured. Be certain that the entire sand area is protected and that the cover is secured with river rocks or another heavy weight so that creatures cannot get underneath.

Sand needs to be raked regularly to remove clumps, debris, and unwanted foreign material. Make it part of the daily routine to rake before and after each outdoor time to keep sand clean, attractive, and moldable. It is not inviting to play in sand that is cluttered with materials or is hard to dig. Use a garden rake to scrape the sand and make it loose and level. Replenish areas that have become too shallow. About twice a year, or more regularly if needed, the sand area needs to be dug deep and turned over with shovels, as it becomes hard and compact over time. You will be amazed at how the volume of sand increases after working it. A new load of sand may not be necessary.

Slipping on sand can be a safety concern. Set a broom nearby to keep paths clear. A lightweight cordless leaf blower works well for blowing sand off of walking surfaces.

The Extra Dimension

After months of planning and preparing, the workday is finally here for the outdoor transformation at a child development center in central California. Upon our arrival, we are greeted by lots of eager volunteer workers—teachers, parents, and family friends—but there are no tree trunks in sight. I am alarmed, because tree trunks are the main element for forming boundaries in two different sand areas. I do not have a plan B. As I am assessing the situation, I hear a warm, friendly greeting, "Miss Lisa, I'm Howard, and I need to know what to do with these tree trunks." Cheri and I follow Howard to the street, and there in a trailer are two of the largest, most beautiful tree trunks we have ever seen. Howard also wants to know if the trunks he collected are good. "What trunks?" I ask. He says, "The ones that I have been bringing and storing behind the school." Cheri and I quickly race to the back of the center, and to our amazement, behind a gated area where trash cans are kept, we discover 80 tree trunks. What a day! Howard is a friend of the child development center, whose profession is cutting down and trimming trees. Everyone needs a Howard in their life.

Tree trunks and logs are one of the easiest ways to add natural beauty and make the biggest aesthetic impact to a play yard, but they can be hard to obtain. Make connections with a tree trimming service, and let family, neighbors, and friends know that you need tree trunks. Tree trunks of all kinds work well, except some pines, which are sappy. Trunks cut 18 inches or less in height do not need to have ground protection underneath them. Varying stump height adds to the visual appeal. Secure trunks and logs in a base such as sand, dirt, or gravel so that they do not wobble. Put your adult weight on top of each stump to test stability. The top surface can be covered with a clear protective sealant to prolong use, but it is not necessary. Trunks need to be replaced periodically, as they do rot. Occasionally trunks have an open end or hole that is perfect for planting a plant.

Feed troughs are upcycled into a sand table.

A shelf underneath is perfect for accessibility and storage.

Small garden shovels are sturdy for digging sand.

Infant/Toddler Sand Zone Ideas

Providing opportunities for infants and toddlers to experience the open-ended exploration of sand and its properties is important. From an early age, sand areas are an ideal place for infants and toddlers to direct their own learning and investigations. Sand play is most appropriate for mobile infants and toddlers, although with supervision younger infants find wiggling and burying bare feet in dry sand intriguing. Buckets, containers, scoops, abalone and scallop shells, large stones, sanded planks, and pieces of smooth wood all enhance experimentation. Consider a small, contained sand area for younger children, as they are not as physically active as preschoolers.

Chapter 11
Water Zones

The sensory delight of water play attracts the attention of Alexa (age three) and Diana (age three), who are both dressed in Princess Elsa attire, from the Disney movie Frozen. "You can have more than one Elsa you know," reports Diana. Apparently, Elsa princesses are captivated by water even when it is not frozen. The princesses become fascinated with the water's trajectory as it travels down the rain gutters and cascades below into the galvanized catch basins. Diana fills a plastic container the size of a mayonnaise jar with water and pours it into a gutter mounted to the water wall at medium height. She watches the water spill off the gutter's edge. Alexa places her hands under the gushing stream. Water spraying on her face does not distract her. She watches the water's movement with great intensity. She shifts her attention to pouring along with Diana and picks up another container. The girls pour  *repeatedly into gutters and track the water as it travels down in serpentine fashion, changes directions, and flows into the large tubs at the base. Pouring begins slowly and methodically, then gets faster and faster. Diana stretches her arms up high to pour water into the top gutter. Her reach is not quite high enough. Water squirts on her and falls into a central gutter. She laughs, scoops another container of water from the catch basin, and adjusts her stretch by standing on her tiptoes. Once again, water splashes her as it falls to the ground. Her strategy shifts, and she pulls over a step stool. She climbs on top of the stool and easily pours water into the top gutter. The girls test and retest their ideas of flow and motion as they pour water into gutters at varying heights. Through this water experience, Alexa and Diana become engineers and scientists and actively develop foundational thinking skills that guide their understanding of the world around them.*

The Value of Water Zones

Children can get the most joy from the simplest things. Whether jumping into puddles on a rainy day, squirting a garden hose, splashing in a fountain, or playing in the bathtub, children love water. Water is an essential natural element for play yards that offers hours of captivating play. Children can make mud pies or wash dishes in the outdoor kitchen, paint with water on a concrete pathway, or float driftwood in a pool of water in the sand. A specially designed water area conveys that investigating water is important work. Intriguing materials combined with children's inquisitive nature make the area a perfect space to explore water in multiple ways, foster curiosity, and deepen understanding of water's properties.

Schema Learning

Transporting: carrying water

Transforming: adding dirt, color, soap, or ice to water

Trajectory: pouring water in gutters, tubing, or funnels

Rotation: watching water rotate in water wheels or from the motion of eggbeaters or wire whisks

Enclosing/enveloping: filling containers

Connecting/disconnecting: fastening hoses, tubing, and pipes and taking them apart

Water Zones to Foster Learning

1. Enhancing Social and Emotional Competencies

During water play children acquire important social skills as they play together, compromise, and share space, equipment, and accessories. Children may move from parallel play (playing alongside someone) to collaborative play (playing with someone). For example, Andrew connects a funnel to a clear piece of tubing and inserts the tube's opposite end inside an empty dish detergent bottle. He repetitively pours cups of water into the funnel. Standing across the water table is Dana, who is focused on filling and emptying containers. The children work in parallel fashion. After several minutes, Dana glances up and pours a container of water into Andrew's funnel. Andrew smiles. He holds the funnel as Dana pours water into it. The two children now work together to fill the bottle. Their ability to work effectively as a team will be helpful in the future as they collaborate with others and when they enter the workforce as adults.

The social skills of Jaxon, Sam, and Eli increase as they play together at a water play center that has a waterfall streambed. They work as a team to fill and pour buckets of water into a large container at the top of the streambed. Then they place large rocks on each tier of the waterfall streambed. The boys work with energy and drive to make a riverbed for fish together. As Eli places on one more rock, Sam pulls out the rubber plug in the water container, releasing water to flow down the streambed. Jaxon shouts, "Wait! The fish!" and places his hands at the streambed's base to stop the water. Eli quickly grabs a large bucket and sets it to catch the stream of water. As the bucket fills, a second bucket replaces it, followed by a third, fourth, and fifth bucket. The boys create an assembly line to carry full buckets of water to the streambed's top and dump water into the large container. The cycle continues to keep water in the streambed for the pretend fish.

Few activities are quite as relaxing and therapeutic as playing in water. Children unwind and calm down as they run their fingers through water, squeeze it from a bottle, and fill containers by submerging them. Simple actions such as pouring water from container to container hold children's attention for long periods of time and increase their ability to self-regulate. Harry sits on the ground with a pitcher of water and several large plastic cups situated between his outstretched legs. Holding the pitcher with both hands, he pours water into three cups. He sets the pitcher down, grasps the rim of one cup with his right hand to steady it, and uses his left hand to pour into the wide opening of another cup—most of the water makes it in. He continues pouring as water spills over the cup's brim. Harry's focus is on pouring and the trajectory of the water. He pours water from the pitcher into cups until the pitcher is empty and then pours water from the cups back into the pitcher to begin again. Water play is also an outlet for overexcited children to release tension and energy. Splashing or slapping water or using strong muscles to squeeze water from a sponge or squeeze bottle can be appropriate ways for children to express their anger, irritation, or frustration.

2. Enhancing Language and Communication Competencies

As children explore water, they have opportunities to learn and use rich vocabulary. Children acquire names for water tools such as funnels, sieves, eggbeaters, basters, whisks, and pitchers. Descriptive language increases as children talk about the size, shape, and color of containers, and actions, including *rotating, pouring, flowing, squeezing, plunging,* and *swishing*. For instance, as Camila and Aria explore the water table, they talk about how the water feels wet and warm but yesterday it was cold. Aria mentions how the water drips when she lifts her hands. Camila drops a rock from up high and comments about the "gigantic splash and ripples." The girls create patterns in the water with sticks and express how they can make wavy, zig-zag, and circular lines. Zachary runs up to the girls with a huge grin on his face and announces that he is drenched. Water play experiences also invite children to practice communication, express their feelings, make social comments, obtain wants and needs, promote and maintain interactions, and articulate ideas. Diana and Salvador re-create the song "Five Green and Speckled Frogs" when plastic frogs, large rocks, and a big piece of driftwood are added to the water table. Diana manipulates the frogs while Salvador sings the song, "One green speckled frog sat on a hollow log, eating the most delicious [bugs], yum yum. He jumped into the pool, where it's nice and cool, now there are no green speckled frogs." Salvador demonstrates oral expression as he sings the song. He shows a sense of internal rhythm and an awareness of pitch and intonation in his voice.

3. Enhancing Cognitive Competencies

As children investigate water, they learn fundamental scientific processes. At the core of all science is observation. For example, Shizuka, Ollie, and Mia play with plastic squeeze bottles at the water table. As Ollie forcefully squeezes a bottle, a stream of water shoots up and falls onto the concrete path, creating a design. Shizuka and Mia laugh and imitate Ollie's action. The three move to the pathway and begin making squiggly lines on the concrete. Mia's squirt shoots over the path and lands on sand. The children notice that the water marks disappear. Classification occurs as the children determine whether water lines made on surfaces will be visible or vanish. Teacher Michael asks the children to describe what they observed and what they are thinking. He asks them to predict what will happen if water is squirted on gravel. "Let's check it out," shouts Mia, and the children run off to research water squirted onto dirt, bark, and the classroom building. The threesome come back to Michael and report the results of their inquiry. Their discovery leads to more understanding of absorption and evaporation.

Micah discovers buoyancy as he experiments to determine which items sink and float. He is curious about why the pumpkin floats when it is so big and heavy. He repeatedly pushes down on the pumpkin to submerge it, but it floats back up. Water walls, funnels, and clear tubing allow children to understand how water flow works, how to direct or alter the flow, and how to stop it. Joel is fascinated with pouring water into the top rain gutter and watching it run back and forth down the water wall. He experiments to make the water go faster, slower, change directions, and stop.

The water area becomes a laboratory for chemists as children mix solutions and experiment with states of water: ice, liquid, and vapor. For instance, Hazel combines beakers of blue and yellow liquid watercolor into a large container. She swirls the colors together with her hand to reveal a new color. Mason investigates a block of ice added to the water table. He sprinkles rock salt on the ice and then squirts on liquid watercolor to create magnificent ice caverns.

Like sand play, water exploration fosters children's mathematical understanding of comparison, measurement, and estimation. While pouring and filling containers, children classify, compare, and contrast things that are smaller or bigger, heavier or lighter, more or less, same or different, and empty or full. Provisioning the water area with standard and nonstandard measuring materials affords children opportunities to investigate volume. How many cups of water does it take to fill up a coffee can, quart jug, or half-gallon bottle? Marni's awareness of weight deepens as she discovers that a half-full container of water weighs less than a full one. Kevin and Todd learn about length as they squirt water from spray bottles. They adjust the bottle nozzles so that water comes out as a solid stream. As their fingers squeeze the triggers, water jets out with great force. A game begins to see who can spray the farthest. Children submerge their hands in water and experience temperature. In the morning, the water table is in the shade and the water is cool. After naptime, the water table is in the sun and feels like bathwater. Marni exhibits an ability to estimate as she adds rocks to a bowl that is half full of water. She guesses how more many rocks are needed before water spills over the bowl's rim.

4. Enhancing Physical Competencies

Children's large- and small-muscle strength increases through experiences with water. Large muscles are used to lift, carry, and dump big containers of water and pump the handle on a hand water pump. Derek and William work to fill a metal tub with water. It is physically demanding but satisfying as they drop a large dump truck into their truck wash.

Small-motor skills and hand-eye coordination develop as children scoop and pour water, rotate an eggbeater, turn a faucet on and off, wring a washcloth, squeeze a turkey baster, and pull the plug in the water table.

Jessica is absorbed in washing pots and pans from the outdoor kitchen. She swirls her hand in the water and then cleans the pots with a scrub brush. Different water tools require various grips. Squirting spray bottles, squeezing bottles of water, painting water on different surfaces, and stirring water all help develop finger and hand muscles.

Teacher Lisa has taken wide-mouth plastic jars and pierced holes into the sides with an ice pick. She places the containers next to the water table. Zoey is the first child to submerge one of the jars. As she pulls it up by the rim, water unexpectedly starts to squirt out from the holes. Zoey squeals at the discovery. She dunks the jar underwater again and this time lifts it by grasping the jar's sides with both hands. She swings her arms around to show Lisa what is happening. Water jets from the holes and falls onto the ground. Zoey is joined by Aaron and Jason, who have come to see what all the excitement is about. The three children use a variety of hand grips to manipulate the jars as they repeatedly plunge the jars and raise them up.

5. Enhancing Expressive Arts

The open-ended nature of water allows for imaginative ideas. Versatile materials in the water area encourage children to use them in resourceful ways. For example, a stick might make ripples in water, serve as a fishing pole, or bring a floating container closer. Jonathan pretends that a floating container of water is a sinking boat about to be destroyed by a rainstorm. He creates a storm by pouring water through a sieve. The boat capsizes as it fills with showering water. Now his play shifts to a rescue mission.

Adding props or small inhabitants to water can encourage dramatic play. Whales, dolphins, or sharks may stimulate stories of danger under the sea. Submarines, boats, and ice add another element of action. Mermaids may inspire fantasy play. Salvador transforms green water into an alligator swamp. Derek and William turn a water tub with bubbles into a truck wash while Jessica uses one for washing dishes. Diana pretends to bathe her baby doll in the bubbles and later washes doll clothes in the soapy mixture.

Essential Components: What Every Water Zone Needs

Space: Consider the types of equipment and furniture you will include to determine the area needed. The space does not need to be big, as children will be standing at the table or water wall most of the time. Position furniture so that children can access as many sides of the water table as possible. More socialization opportunities and fewer space issues occur when children are across from each other and have more room to play.

The water area needs to be on flat ground so that water stays level inside tubs. Locate the area on a surface with good drainage, such as gravel or bark. A concrete surface also works well, as water will evaporate or run off. Avoid placing a water table on grass, as excessive spilled water and high traffic on wet grass will kill it. A nearby water tap makes it easy to refill jugs and replenish water.

The area can be amazingly simple. A commercially purchased water table or play center can be nice, but children find buckets, dish tubs, or large containers of water just as satisfying. Individual dish tubs, concrete mixing tubs, large basins, or plastic containers that sit on a low bench, table, or tree stump work well for water play. Shallow containers may also be placed directly on the ground for infants.

Water zone before

The stucco wall of the center is a blank slate.

Water zone after

This water zone consists of outdoor storage benches with wall panels and shelves. Large black tubs sit on the benches. The water faucet is located on the building wall to the side of the left bench. Children can independently access the water tubs on three sides. Organizing filling and dumping materials on hooks uses the vertical storage space. Extra items are stored on top shelves out of children's reach, but shelf height can be adjusted lower for children to access materials if desired. Natural elements such as stones, seashells, and driftwood are stored in open-frame wire containers so that water will drain out.

Top Tips for Designing Water Zones

1. Use upcycled furniture for water play; there is no need for a commercial water table.
2. Position furniture so children can access multiple sides of the water table.
3. Arrange materials for filling and dumping so they are organized and accessible.
4. Make natural elements such as stones and seashells available to children.
5. Use open frame containers so water will drain out.
6. Use vertical storage space for tubing and measuring cups.
7. Make sure the water source is nearby and water can be independently accessed

Enhancing water zones: A key to a successful water zone is having water that children can independently access. One of the best options is a plastic water dispenser with a spigot. These jugs also have a wide opening for filling and cleaning and an easy-to-carry handle. Set jugs on the water table, shelves, or benches in the area at the children's level. Teach children how to use the spigot and provide guidelines for refilling dispensers. My experience has been that children are more careful with water consumption when they oversee getting it. Adults are always responsible for filling or supervising the filling of dispensers. Foreign debris added to the water clogs and destroys the spigot. I have observed children opening the lid and pouring dirt inside the jug to see the transformation. It is an exceptionally good research investigation that has a bad outcome for water jugs. Galvanized beverage dispensers with a spigot are available but are quite expensive.

Water Zone Tools and Materials

Water Containers
Basins
Concrete mixing tubs
Dish tubs for
   individual play
Galvanized beverage
   dispenser
Large plastic tubs
Plastic dispenser with
   spigot
Utility or laundry sink
Water table

Fill-and-Empty Materials
Buckets
Containers with nar-
   row openings
Containers with wide
   openings
Dry measuring cups
Graduated cylinders
Ladles
Liquid measuring cups

Trajectory Materials
Bamboo water pipe
Basters
Clear tubing
Colanders
Containers with holes
Funnels of various
   sizes
Hand pump
Pipettes
Pitchers
Rain gutters
Sieves
Spray bottles
Squeeze bottles
Strainers
Watering cans

Transforming Materials
Dish detergent
Ice
Liquid watercolor
Paintbrushes
Paint rollers
Scrub brushes
Sponges

Rotating Materials
Eggbeaters
Water wheels
Wire whisks

Connecting and Disconnecting Materials
Clear tubing
Connectors
Funnels
Pipe tubes

Natural Materials (good for sink and float)
Corks
Driftwood
Rocks
Seashells
Twigs

Pretend Play Materials
Boats
Dishes

Dolls and baby
   clothes
Miniature rubber
   animals (frogs, fish,
   whales)

Water Wall Bases
Fence
Lattice
Plywood
Side of a building
   or shed
Wood pallet

Water Wall Materials
Buckets
Clear tubing
Fittings
Funnels
Hoses
Pipes
Plastic jugs or bottles
Rain gutters
Tubes

Graduated cylinders foster children's mathematical understanding of comparison, measurement, and estimation.

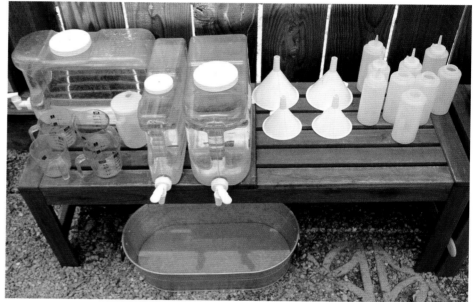

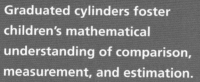

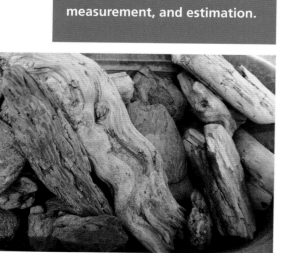

Storage and Organization

A shelf underneath a water table or bench provides accessible storage. Low outdoor storage shelves are another good option. Place materials such as driftwood, stones, and seashells in wire baskets on the shelves. Items such as containers or measuring cups can sit directly on shelves. Consider mounting materials on a wall panel, trellis, pegboard, or pallet. Items such as clear tubing and measuring cups can hang from hooks. Funnels or containers can sit on wall-mounted shelves.

A low-level water station was created for young toddlers. The tub can be placed on the ground for infants to access water.

Cleaning and Maintaining the Space

Have towels handy for easy cleanup. Be alert, as water spilled on some floor surfaces can be a slipping hazard and needs to be addressed immediately. Check your state guidelines for policies about using and cleaning water tables. As a rule, water containers and materials need to be emptied, sanitized with a bleach solution (2 teaspoons of bleach to 1 gallon of water) and left to air-dry after use. Sanitize materials and accessories and turn them over to dry. Smaller pieces can be placed upside down in open-framed baskets to air-dry. While cleaning and organizing water materials, inspect pieces and replace or repair any broken items. Plastic jugs do not hold up well in hot sun and may need to be replaced every year. A galvanized jug with a spigot is a sustainable option.

Water Stewardship

Because water is such a precious natural resource, modeling good stewardship of water is critical. The goal is to use as little potable water as possible, which is a challenge when children love water play so much. Implement a water conservation plan by capturing rainwater to use for play. Place buckets, rain barrels, or tubs on the ground to catch water that flows from gutters, and teach children how to reuse it. Recycle used play water to water gardens, trees, plants, and grass. Once water is turned off at the tap, remove the outdoor faucet handle from the spigot so that water may not be turned on until you bring back the handle.

The Extra Dimension

An old-fashioned hand pump is a wonderful addition to any water area. Nothing compares to the joy children experience as water miraculously emerges. Children delight in repeatedly pumping the handle and gain a sense of accomplishment in making water flow. They also learn about gravity, water flow, and how a pump works. Websites sell a wide variety of hand pumps designed for children's playgrounds. Hand pumps may be purchased at a specialty tool or farm supply and equipment store. Some hand pumps are mounted on a stainless-steel tub, some draw water from a reservoir, and others connect to a live water supply or rainwater tank. Certain pumps are suited for water and sand play while others are appropriate for large creek beds and water channels. Some pumps have a circulating system to preserve water. If you are handy, you can design a way to mount a pump on a platform that accesses a water source. Handle and spout designs vary as well. For example, some spouts have a hook that

helps children fill buckets. Know that commercial hand pump systems can be exceptionally pricey, and there can be challenges with water flow and clogging. Select a pump that has excellent reviews for functionality and durability. Choose a design that has no pinch points and prevents children from pouring sand into the top.

Supporting Equitable Learning

- Provide multiple levels of water play, such as tubs of water on the ground for children who cannot stand at a water table.
- Make material adaptations to support all children's participation. For example, use a water table that is specially designed for wheelchair users to access, or arrange a low gutter and funnel on the water wall for children who cannot reach higher gutters.
- Allow children to use materials and try out new skills in unusual ways.
- Provide materials that challenge various levels of skills, such as basters, eggbeaters, squeeze bottles, water wheels, pumps, and plastic tubing.

Rain is created by pouring water into the top holes of the pipe. Water falls through tiny holes in the bottom of the pipe.

Low gutters on the water wall allow toddlers to successfully pour water.

Children have mastered using syringes, which they call "blasters."

Infant/Toddler Water Zone Ideas

Water play is a pleasurable and satisfying experience for infants and toddlers. Older infants who can support their core can use their hands to slap water in a baking tray during supervised tummy time. Infants who sit reasonably well can splash and explore water and accessories in shallow containers. Provide funnels, scoops, and small containers that are easy to grasp. Include natural materials to explore, such as driftwood, stones, and seashells. Low, sturdy water tables are perfect for infants and toddlers who can pull themselves up to stand. Tubes and gutters can be adjusted to lower heights so that toddlers can reach them.

Chapter 12
Cozy Spaces and Hiding Places

Salvador (age four) picks up one of his favorite books, Room on the Broom *by Julia Donaldson. He snuggles against the pillows in the cozy area and begins to tell the story out loud. As he flips the pages and tells his version, several children gather to listen. Salvador quietly continues. He knows the story well because it has been read to him many times. He points to pictures and uses language to imitate the story as he plays "teacher" and reads to his friends. It is a special experience as he shares his interest in books and reading. As he finishes reading, his dad arrives to take him home for the weekend. On Monday morning, Salvador appears quiet and reserved. Teacher Cheri warmly welcomes him and asks about his weekend. He stands silently, looks around, but does not engage with any activities. Cheri encourages him to join the clay or trajectory work that he found so satisfying on Friday, but he does not move. Cheri gently takes Salvador's hand and whispers, "Sal, come with me. I have something to show you that I think you will like." She leads Salvador over to the cozy area under the evergreen and sequoia trees. There in the book rack is* Room on the Broom. *Salvador smiles. As Cheri reads the story to him, he begins to relax and settle in. Every child is different at school. One child may be ready to play immediately upon arrival, while another may need more time, particularly after a weekend. Spending quiet time in a cozy space can be the perfect way for a child to slowly transition from home to school.*

The Value of Cozy Spaces and Hiding Places

A glance around the yard reveals lots of energetic and vigorous play, but you will also notice children who are sitting relaxed and content under the shade of a tree or inside an open barrel. Outdoor play offers children all types of active activities, but outdoor environments also need to include quiet spaces for children who are overwhelmed, stressed, tired, or just want to take a break and pace their interactions. Taking time to reflect, observe, and rest is essential for children's well-being. Children need relaxed, quiet time that requires less initiative and activity on their part. Cozy spaces and hiding places are areas where children can enjoy a quiet moment alone or with a friend. The space is small, partially enclosed, and has room for only one or two children. Cozy spaces and hiding places are protected, peaceful, and safe refuges for children to find solitude, relax, or self-regulate. Play materials in the space are typically manipulatives, games, and books. Offering tranquil outdoor spaces allows children the opportunity to self-select a private space to enjoy calm exploration.

Schema Learning

Schema learning in a cozy space will depend on the loose parts that are available in the space.

Transporting: carrying loose parts to and from the space

Transforming: watching seasonal changes in the environment, such as leaves turning color; using small loose parts to create designs and representations

Rotation: spinning tops, hanging mobiles

Enclosing/enveloping: covering oneself or wrapping a doll with a blanket or scarf; wrapping yarn around a dowel; climbing into a box or tent

Connecting/disconnecting: twisting nuts and bolts together; connecting lids and jars; lacing; stretching and linking elastic bands on geoboards; taking a puzzle apart; pulling apart connecting items such as magnetic pieces

Cozy Spaces and Hiding Places to Foster Learning

1. Enhancing Social and Emotional Competencies

In a cozy space, children gain emotional competency by recognizing their feelings and learning how to respond appropriately. When a child is feeling anxious, overwhelmed, sad, or stressed, a cozy space can be a refuge to regain control of emotions and engage in quiet reflection. Solitude lets children recharge their bodies and minds, self-regulate, and handle stress. Privacy and time away from group experiences is essential for a child's mental health. For example, Diana often likes to be by herself in the outdoor cozy area, relaxing on a pillow while reading a book. When finished, she watches the play yard activity for a moment and then starts to explore on her own. Micah sits quietly in the cozy area and puts a puzzle together. He can focus without interruption in the private space. Emily and Stephanie are special friends who enjoy each other's company and find large groups tiring and overwhelming. The girls find opportunities to share the quiet, relaxing cozy area nestled in a corner of the yard. Playing together in the intimate setting helps them develop friendship and social skills. While having a tea party, they develop capacities for social skills such as listening to each other, sharing, managing disagreements, taking turns, and cooperating. The girls create an elegant table setting together with enamel camping mugs and plates. They collaborate in decorating their quilt tabletop with rose petals and sprigs of rosemary. A menu of tree cookie biscuits, acorn mints, chocolate-dipped pine cones, and raspberry tea is negotiated. Once everything is prepared, Emily and Stephanie take turns greeting and serving their stuffed animal guests. The party is filled with lots of fun and laughter in addition to the tasty and pretty treats.

2. Enhancing Language and Communication Competencies

In cozy spaces, children can expand language and communication competencies through uninterrupted, meaningful conversations. Under the shade of a tunnel created with reed garden fencing, Diana, Alexa, and teacher Cheri sit on benches and engage in rich conversation. Their lengthy dialogue centers around scary topics, including germs, thunder, monsters, and aliens. Talking about germs has been a dominant topic because the children have just returned to Cheri's care after sheltering in place from the COVID-19 pandemic. Their conversation changes to thunderstorms that occurred over the weekend as Diana states, "What makes thunder is electricity." Alexa expresses how "clouds are dark, dark, dark and dangerous because there are monsters in them." Diana reports, "Monsters come out at Halloween." The conversation shifts to a shadow that Alexa saw in her bedroom that was a monster. Alexa uses descriptive words to express what the monster looked like (orange and comfy). Diana explains, "Monsters come out of the moon." Alexa clarifies, "Only aliens live on the moon." When challenged by teacher Cheri to explain how aliens get on the moon, Diana says, "They drive on their alien rocket ships." Throughout this fascinating conversation, teacher Cheri supports the girls' development of language skills through sustained, meaningful, and in-depth dialogue. She encourages the girls to describe monsters and aliens and challenges statements they make to reveal their thinking. She guides them in using reciprocal communication when both girls talk at the same time or one dominates the extended conversation.

3. Enhancing Cognitive Competencies

Loose parts placed in the cozy area naturally lend themselves to learning math concepts. Acorns, seashells, eucalyptus pods, pine cones, and sea glass encourage patterning, comparing, classifying, counting, and measuring. Ryan has been working on the cozy area platform with natural materials. Large round shapes (tree cookies), long skinny shapes (cinnamon sticks), and small pointed shapes (seashells) offer contrasting shapes and sizes for him to create interesting patterns. He can sort items according to color, shape, size, texture, properties, or function depending on the materials' attributes. Today, after making a spiral of alternating pieces on a round reed place mat, he arranges acorns into small and large and then into those with caps and those without. Ryan declares, "The ones with caps are dangerous because they can explode." Ryan shows an understanding of number and quantity as he accurately counts out 10 acorns for himself and 10 for Mark to keep the bad guys away.

Sheila distinguishes between different sizes and experiences seriation, first as she lines up plastic graduated hair rollers in an orderly, progressive row, and later as she fits the plastic cylinders inside each other. She places one roller on each of her 10 fingers, exhibiting one-to-one correspondence. Isabella recognizes similarities and differences as she sorts squares of fabrics from an old upholstery sample book into piles of solids, plaids, stripes, and flowers. Next, she lines up fabric squares to measure the width of the platform. She estimates as she announces, "Oh wow, it's eight long. I'm going to need more to go this way [referring to the length]."

As Ryan, Mia, and Isabella play with loose parts in the cozy area, they will grow to see mathematics as natural and significant. They are gaining a solid understanding of math concepts and ideas through their concrete exploration of materials, which will help them in future learning.

4. Enhancing Physical Competencies

A variety of manipulatives help strengthen and refine small motor skills, including pincer grip, squeezing, gripping, rotating, eye-hand coordination, and bilateral coordination. Pincer grasps are used to pick up buttons or colored stones to place in a muffin tin or transfer to wooden bowls. The pincer grip is increased further by using toast, ice, or silicone tongs to pick up and transfer items. Turning the pages in a book requires a pincer grasp. Hayley (10 months) improves squeezing and gripping muscles as she explores loofas, felted wool balls, pom-pom puff balls, and silk scarves. Nuts, bolts, jars, and lids support wrist rotation, eye-hand coordination, and bilateral coordination. Threading pipe cleaners through wooden wheels with holes, lacing shoestrings through large buttons, and inserting cloth napkins inside napkin rings increases eye-hand coordination and bilateral coordination. Catrina discovers that wooden thread spools and smooth stones are perfect for stacking and balancing. Commercial materials such as geoboards, tangrams, and puzzles are good for developing and refining small motor control as children stretch rubber bands and fit small pieces into place.

5. Enhancing Expressive Arts

A cozy space can be a perfect location for creative storytelling. Puppets, block play people, and miniature vehicles placed in the private space can inspire imaginative stories. Farm or jungle animals combined with loose parts are naturally appealing. Teachers can also set up props for narrating well-known stories. As Evan walks past the cozy area, he is invited by Andrew to join him. Positioned on the platform in front of Andrew are props to support the telling of "The Three Billy Goats Gruff": a family of three goats, a bumpy gourd (the troll), a brown place mat, green moss, a blue scarf, and a hollow tree log tunnel. Having heard the story multiple times, they reenact it using the correct sequence with lots of sound effects as the goats' hooves *trip-trap* across the bridge and the troll roars, "Who's that tripping over my bridge?" A dramatic scream echoes out as the troll falls from the bridge, followed by a loud splash.

The cozy area is also a quiet space for older preschoolers to engage in handwork such as weaving or stitchery. Yarns, ribbons, collage strips, and other natural materials form creations with intriguing textures, patterns, and colors. An attractive display of natural objects or appealing glass stones invites children to create patterns and arrangements that demonstrate their sensitivity to beauty. Practicing handwork and making designs helps young children develop a strong imagination.

Essential Components: What Every Cozy Space and Hiding Place Needs

Space: Position cozy areas in a quiet zone of the play yard away from the hustle and noise of active spots. The space should be tucked away and sheltered from distractions and traffic pathways. Be resourceful when designing cozy spaces. They may be simple and small. Cozy areas can be created on platforms, patios, or porches; under natural or manufactured canopies or lean-to shelters; and in tunnels, cardboard boxes, tents, or old bathtubs. A platform size of 6 feet by 4 feet works well for a couple of children or a teacher and child. Patio cushions can be a perfect choice. They are soft, comfortable, and available in a variety of sizes and colors. Many have removable, machine-washable covers for easy care. Consider a rug with pillows nestled in a quiet nook, or upcycle an old rowboat.

Work space: Cozy areas should be designed so children feel hidden from view yet still maintain visibility for adult supervision. Redwood or cedar garden lattice for walls and fence post caps on corner posts add beauty, enhance the space, and give an element of privacy. Draping a space with a canopy netting gives children the illusion of privacy while being transparent enough for adults to see through. Lattice panels provide a partial screen that enables supervision. Sheer outdoor curtains, shower curtains, bedsheets, or drop cloths can bring softness, warmth, and privacy to a cozy space. Textiles can be suspended from a tree, fence, clothesline, or patio rafter. Barriers can be created with low shelving units in a corner space or against a fence or building wall.

Natural or living canopies such as shade trees and climbing vines can provide the perfect secluded space. Natural canopies may also be created. Teacher Morgan created a living hut by planting willows and guiding the branches into the shape of a dome as they grew. The hut is a secret hiding space for the children in her program. Instructions for creating and maintaining living willow structures can be found on the internet.

Manufactured canopies include playhouses, parachutes, lean-to shelters designed with fabric, natural reed garden fencing, or netting. Heavy-duty corrugated metal designed for roofing is a rustic option. An umbrella with pillows underneath can make an intimate hideaway. Private spaces may also be made by placing cushions inside a 36-inch diameter industrial pipe or setting up pillows underneath reed garden fencing draped over a frame.

Cozy space before

The area under the patio overhang is underutilized, with spaces for adults to sit and a few random building blocks. Teacher Nina's desire is to create defined play spaces that can be used during hot and rainy weather.

Cozy space after

A carpenter built a three-sided cozy space on the patio. Wooden planks are laid in varying directions to provide interest, texture, and beauty. Pillows add soft textural elements. Fabric stored in a wicker basket is available for children to drape and secure with clamps attached to the top of the frame. This space is frequently used as a theater stage as well as a space to relax.

Top Tips for Designing Cozy Spaces and Hiding Places

1. Contained sides provide privacy.
2. An open front allows visibility for supervision.
3. A patio cover offers protection from sun and rain.
4. Textural elements of pillows, draped fabric, and cushions add softness and comfort.
5. Providing loose parts gives children items to quietly explore.

Enhancing cozy spaces: A cozy area needs a calm and peaceful atmosphere that nurtures and supports children. The space should give the message that this is a comfortable, safe zone to relax, explore materials without distraction, or enjoy some solitude. Consider the space's function and design by incorporating elements that children find soothing, engaging, and calming, and that draw them into the space. Soft textural elements such as pillows, cushions, rugs, comforters, and blankets add tranquility and create a sense of calm. Draping fabric above the space or at the entrance is another way to add softness. Create coziness by adding plants, books, and warm tones with natural wood. Include rustic accents such as a tree stump stool or table. Elevate the space with sensory accents of wind chimes and soothing scents of lavender.

Cozy Spaces Tools and Materials

Creating Softness and Privacy
Bedsheets
Blankets
Body pillows
Canopies
Canopy netting

Comforters
Crib mattress
Cushions
Drop cloths
Fabrics
Large umbrellas
Parachutes
Pillows

Porch swing on the ground
Quilts
Rugs
Sheer outdoor curtains
Shower curtains

Loose Parts

Cozy areas do not need to be limited to looking at books. Consider rotating quiet manipulatives and include loose parts that support positioning, small building, designing, imagining, classifying, patterning, comparing, counting, connecting, disconnecting, and inserting.

Acorns
Bottle caps
Buttons
CDs
Cedar rings
Cinnamon sticks
Corks
Driftwood (small pieces)
Eucalyptus pods
Film canisters
Glass stones
Jar lids
Keys
Leaves
Liquid amber tree or sweetgum tree balls
Maple wood rings
Marker caps
Metal washers
Pieces of old jewelry

Pine cones
Pom-poms
Sea glass
Seashells
Seedpods
Sticks
Stones
Tiles
Tree blocks
Tree cookies
Wooden thread spools

Connecting and Disconnecting
Bark
Clothespins
Combs
Hangers
Jars and lids
Nuts and bolts
Ribbon

Rope
Scarf hangers
Shoelaces
Sock hangers
String
Velcro rollers
Wire
Yarn
Zip ties

Inserting
Bowls
Boxes
Bracelets
Candle holder with holes
Coffee pod holder
Colanders
Containers

Cups
Dowels
Felted rings
Hair donuts
Hair scrunchies
Keys and locks
Letter holder
Maple wood rings
Metal canning rings
Napkin rings
Paper towel holder
Pipe cleaners
Plate holder
Puzzles
Scarf holder
Tin cans
Tissue box
Tubes

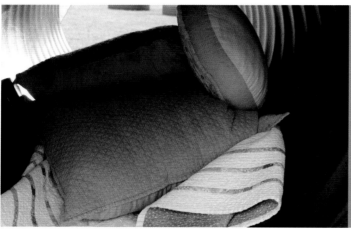

Pillows and a comforter placed inside a large drainpipe offer a cozy place to relax.

Storage and Organization

Pillows, cushions, or other cozy items may need to be brought inside at the end of each day for protection from the elements and vandalism. Manipulatives for a cozy area are typically stored inside a classroom, home, or storage shed. Teachers select materials based on children's interests and bring them out at the beginning of each day. Organization in a cozy area can be as simple as placing materials in a tray or basket or staging materials on the ground. If low shelving units define the space, they can store manipulatives. Too many items can be overstimulating, limit work space, and produce a sense of chaos and disorderliness.

A screen behind the platform provides privacy and beauty.

Cleaning and Maintaining the Space

Cushions, pillows, blankets, and other soft items need to be washed or replaced periodically. It is helpful to select pillows and cushions with covers that can be removed for easy cleaning. Items need to be stored inside or covered during inclement weather for protection. A handheld leaf blower is useful for removing dust and debris. Identify and rotate manipulatives according to children's developmental level and interests.

The Extra Dimension

Dog beds are a good, simple option for cozy spaces. Many dog beds feature plush, comfy surfaces. Some have bolster walls that add security and comfort, while others are open for children to stretch out. They come in multiple sizes to fit into just the right nook. Because they are made for dogs, they are durable, and many have waterproof covers that are removable for convenient cleaning. Drape the bed with a soft fleece blanket that feels comfy for snuggling. Enhance the visual appeal with accent pillows that children can hold or lean up against.

Supporting Equitable Learning

- Add a variety of manipulatives that increase in complexity to support differing developmental levels.
- Create a quiet, simple space for children with sensory sensitivities; features may include soft natural lighting, a diffuser, or weighted blanket (calming); noise-canceling headphones or a sound machine (auditory); a hanging chair or bouncing ball (vestibular); and textured balls, loofas, and fidgets (tactile).
- Add loose parts that vary in weight, size, and texture. Loose parts have a built-in tolerance for error (there is not a right or wrong way to use them).
- Incorporate puzzles with knobs that are easy to grasp, insert, and remove.
- Replace shoelaces with pipe cleaners or wooden dowels to make insertion easier.
- Use both large and small versions of manipulatives, such as supersized and regular-sized thread spools.
- Create cozy spaces adapted for mobility so that they are accessible for all children. For instance, design spaces on the ground or provide wide access, grab bars, or a ramp.
- Be certain that platforms or furniture in the space are heavy and stable to prevent tipping.

Teacher Morgan created a living willow hut by planting willow branches and guiding the branches into the shape of a dome as they grew.

Infant/Toddler Cozy Space Ideas

Create a cozy, safe space for infants by placing a soft blanket and pillows on top of a canvas tarp. Choose a location that is away from active play and off to the side. Large pieces of driftwood and pillows can act as borders around the blanket for protection. Place loose parts on the blanket to foster infants' interest in looking, listening, mouthing, grasping, squeezing, pulling, and inserting:

- Sealed plastic bottles filled with items that make different sounds when shaken

- Maple wood rings and silicone cupcake liners and utensils for mouthing

- Dog rope pulls, hacky sack balls, bath loofahs, knotted cloth napkins, scarves tied to wooden rings, and silicone trivet rings for grasping and squeezing

- Scarves placed inside a geometric sphere centerpiece for infants to pull out

- Extra-large buttons and canning rings for infants to insert into a wooden tissue-box cover

- Wooden or wire strainer scoops to pick up felted balls

For toddlers, design cozy spaces with loose parts that support their interest in stacking, inserting, and connecting/disconnecting:

- Smooth countertop tile samples or tree cookies for stacking

- Hair scrunchies, hair bun donuts, wooden and metal rings, and napkin rings for inserting on a wooden or metal paper towel holder

- Round wooden clothespins for inserting into a container

- Self-grip hair rollers for connecting and disconnecting

Appendix A
Be, Do, Become Process

Included here is an example of the Be, Do, Become process. Below are the words generated by teachers at Creative Spirit Learning Center in Fair Oaks, California, as they reflected on children in their outdoor environment.

BE	*DO*		*BECOME*
Angry	Balance	Lead	Accepting
Artistic	Build	Line	Activist
Assertive	Bury	Make	Advocate
Bossy	Capture	Mix	Artistic
Brave	Carry	Observe	Capable
Collaborative	Catch bugs	Paint	Challenger
Controlling	Climb	Plant	Communicator
Curious	Collaborate	Pour	Compassionate
Dirty	Collect	Pull	Confident
Empathetic	Connect	Push	Connected
Energetic	Cover	Rake	Coordinated
Excited	Create	Read	Creative
Failure	Cry	Relocate	Critical thinker
Fearless	Dance	Repel	Discerning
Follower	Design	Run	Empathetic
Frustrated	Destroy	Seek	Environmentalist
Happy	Dig	Sift	Flexible
Inquisitive	Draw	Sing	Happy
Leader	Drive	Sit	Independent
Loud	Dump	Skip	Individual
Messy	Fall	Slash	Knowledgeable
Powerful	Fight	Slide	Outspoken
Powerless	Fill	Sort	Persistent
Proud	Find	Spin	Powerful
Quiet	Fly	Splash	Problem solver
Reflective	Follow	Spray	Protester
Sad	Gallop	Squirt	Researcher
Scared	Garden	Stack	Resilient
Successful	Harvest	Stir	Scientist
	Hide	Swing	Spiritual
	Hose	Take care of	Strong
	Hunt for bugs	Talk	Sure-footed
	Investigate	Throw	Team player
	Jump	Topple	Well rounded
	Laugh	Transform	
		Yell	

Appendix B
Assessing Your Current Outdoor Environment

Outdoor Play Zon	What We Have to Support Play in the Zone	What Loose Parts and Other Items I Would Like to See
Art Studio		
Clay Studio		
Sound Garden		
Mud Kitchen		
Small Worlds		
Construction Zone		
Trajectory Zone		
Large-Motor Zone		
Sand Zone		
Water Zone		
Cozy Space/Hiding Place		
Other Ideas		

Appendix C
Outdoor Zone Materials and Accessories

Art Tools and Materials

Natural Loose Parts
Acorns
Bamboo
Bark
Catalpa pods
Cinnamon sticks
Corn husks
Driftwood
Eucalyptus pods
Flowers (dried)
Leaves
Oak galls
Palm tree bark
Pine cones
Pine needles
Rocks
Sea beans
Sea glass
Seashells
Seed pods
Sticks
Stones
Sycamore balls
Tree cookies
Twigs

Textiles
Burlap
Carpet samples
Fabric squares
Raffia
Ribbon
Shoelaces
String
Twine
Yarn

Tiles
Ceramic
Colored
Glass
Mosaic
Pebbles
Pool
Porcelain
River
Rock
Slate
Stone
Subway
Wall

Metal
Embroidery hoops
Film reels
Keys
Lids
Metal caps
Napkin rings
Nuts and bolts
Rings
Washers

Wood
Beads
Clothespins
Corks
Craft sticks
Embroidery hoops
Floor samples
Napkin rings
Picture frame samples
Scrap wood
Thread spools

Plastic
Beads
Bottle caps
CD cases
Coffee stirrers
Corrugated sheets
Cups
Cylinders
Film canisters
Film spools
Marker caps
Napkin rings
Pipe
Pipe fittings
Tape spools
Tubes
Zip ties

Items to Designate Work Spaces
Acrylic mirrors (12 by 12 inches)
Picture frames
Place mats
Plates
Tiles (12 by 12 inches)
Trays
Wooden cutting boards

Art Materials
Bingo daubers
Cans or bowls for paint
Cans/containers for chalk, brushes, water
Canvas for each child
Chalk
Cleaning cloths
Crates (to hold canvases)
Crayons
Markers
Paint
Paintbrushes
Pastels
Stand for paint cans (tree trunk, crate, small table)
Water tubs for rinsing brushes
Watercolor pencils
Watercolors
Wire

Clay Tools and Materials

Setup Materials
Clay boards or wooden cutting boards
Clay cutter (wire clay cutter, dental floss, string)
Small bucket or tub of water (for children to moisten their sponges or paper towels)
Water holders (sponges, paper towels, small bowls, plastic spray bottle)

Clay Tools
Boxwood tools such as ribs and scrapers (modeling tools for creating fine details and markings)
Forks and spoons
Mallets
Ribbon and wire loop tools
Rolling pins
Wooden dowels

Accessory Materials

Acorns
Combs
Craft sticks/sticks
Eucalyptus pods
Large wooden beads
Nuts, bolts, washers
Old toothbrushes
Seashells
Stones
Wire

Cleanup Materials

Buckets for cleanup water
Cloth towels
Scrapers

Sound Garden Tools and Materials

Items to Strike

Angel food cake pan
Baking sheet
Black corrugated drainage pipe
Bread pan
Broiler rack
Bucket
Bundt pan
Cake pan
Canning rings
Cannoli form tubes
Colander
Cookie sheet
Cooling rack
Corrugated metal roof panel
Fluted tube pan
Gourds
Loaf pan
Metal tray
Muffin pan
Nana bell
Pie pan
Pots and pans
Roasting pan
Serving tray
Springform pan
Tart rings
Tin cans of various sizes

Trash can (metal and rubber)
Trash can lid
Wind chimes
Wooden bowls

Striking Utensils (wood and metal)

Bamboo pieces
Dowel
Ladle
Masher
Mesh strainer
Paint stirrer
Pasta server
Slotted spoon
Spatula
Splatter guard
Spoon
Stick
Stirring spoon
Strainer
Tongs
Whisk

Mud Kitchen Tools and Materials

Kitchenware

Bread pans
Cake pans
Canisters
Colanders
Mixing bowls
Mortar and pestle
Muffin tins
Pie pans
Skillets and saucepans
Small metal creamer pitchers
Strainers
Tin cans

Utensils

Metal spoons
Pancake turners
Potato mashers
Slotted spoons
Spatulas
Wire whisks
Wooden spoons

Small World Tools and Materials

Containers and Bases

Barrel
Bathtub
Birdbath
Boot tray
Box lid
Builder tray
Burl wood or large log
Clay saucers
Colander
Concrete mixing tub
Cookie sheet
Drawer
Flowerpot saucer
Gravel pan
Hollow log
Jelly roll pan
Mud tray
Oil pan
Planter
Raised garden bed
Redwood planter box
Rug
Serving tray
Sheet pan
Suitcase
Tire
Wagon
Wheelbarrow
Window boxes
Wood tray
Wooden barrel

Plants

Basil
Chives
Cilantro
Dill
Mint
Oregano
Parsley
Peppermint
Rosemary
Sage
Strawberries
Succulents
Sweet marjoram
Tarragon
Thyme

Small-World Surfaces

Bark
Basil leaves (dried)
Cocoa mulch
Coconut husk bedding
Corncob bedding
Dill weed (dried)
Dirt
Eucalyptus leaves (dried)
Flowering kale
Forest moss
Glass stones
Gravel
Hay
Kinetic sand
Lavender (dried)
Mint (dried)
Moss
Pebbles
Reindeer moss
Rose buds (dried)
Rosemary (dried)
Sheet moss
Sod
Spanish moss (dried)
Spearmint (dried)
Straw
Wheatgrass

Small-World Loose Parts

Acorns
Branches
Cinnamon sticks
Driftwood
Eucalyptus pods
Leaves
Pine cones
Scarves
Sea beans
Sea glass
Seashells
Seed pods
Spools (wooden)
Sticks
Stones
Tiles
Tree cookies
Twigs
White mulberry root bark

Construction Zone Tools and Materials

Construction Pieces

Bed risers
Black corrugated pipe
Black PVC pipe (4 or 6 inches in diameter cut into 6-, 9-, and 12-inch pieces)
Cove molding (2- to 4-foot lengths)
Ladders (small)
Logs
Milk crates
Pallets
Planks (1 to 6 feet in length)
Pulley system
Redwood blocks (4-by-4-inch posts cut into 4-, 8-, and 12-inch lengths)
Sandbags (4 by 8 inches or 6 by 12 inches)
Sawhorses (mini)
Tires
Tree blocks
Tree trunks
Wood cables
Wood crates
Wood planks
Wood scraps

Loose Parts

Driftwood
Large rocks
Rope
Tin cans
Wood pieces

Trajectory Zone Tools and Materials

Inclines

Black corrugated drainage pipe
Black PVC tubes
Cardboard cove molding
Carpet tubes
Clear PVC tubes
Cove molding (1-, 2-, 3-, and 4-foot lengths)
PVC pipe (4-, 8-, and 12-inch pieces)
Rubber base molding
Sturdy cardboard
Vinyl rain gutters
White PVC tubes
Wood ramps

Bases to Support Inclines

Barrels
Boulders
Concrete blocks
Crates
Mini sandbags
Mini sawhorses
Pallets
Tree trunks
Wood frames with dowels
Wood frames with rope
Wooden spools

Things That Roll

Balls of all types (whiffle, handball, plastic baseball, ball pit, and wooden balls)
Canning rings
Hula hoops
Maple rings
Napkin rings
Pine cones
Spools
Stones
Tires
Tree cookies
Wheels

Things That Pour

Dirt
Gravel
Sand
Water

Large-Motor Zone Materials

Barrels
Benches
Boulders
Corrugated drainpipe (4 inches wide)
Logs
Milk crates
Mini ladders
Mini sawhorses
Pallets
Planks or walking boards (narrow planks: 6 inches by 8 to 10 feet; and wide planks: 1 foot by 6 to 8 feet)
Platforms or sturdy wooden boxes for jumping
Solid wood crates
Tires (car and truck)
Tree trunks
Wood cable spools

Sand Zone Tools and Materials

Digging Tools

Kitchen utensils
Scoops (metal)
Shovels
Spades
Spoons (metal)
Sticks
Trucks, diggers, bulldozers

Natural Resources

Abalone shells
Bark
Coconut shells
Large rocks
Scallop shells
Seashells
Stones (small and large)
Tree trunks
Wood

Containers and Construction Tools

Funnels
Gutters
Metal buckets—various sizes
Muffin tins
Pie pans
Pipes
Ramps
Sheets of heavy plastic for building lakes, rivers, and dams
Sieves
Tin cans
Tubes

Water Zone Tools and Materials

Water Containers

Basins
Concrete mixing tubs
Dish tubs for individual play
Galvanized beverage dispenser
Large plastic tubs
Plastic dispenser with spigot
Utility or laundry sink
Water table

Fill-and-Empty Materials

Buckets
Containers with narrow openings
Containers with wide openings
Dry measuring cups
Graduated cylinders
Ladles
Liquid measuring cups

Trajectory Materials

Bamboo water pipe
Basters
Clear tubing
Colanders
Containers with holes
Funnels of various sizes
Hand pump
Pipettes
Pitchers
Rain gutters
Sieves
Spray bottles
Squeeze bottles
Strainers
Watering cans

Transforming Materials
Dish detergent
Ice
Liquid watercolor
Paintbrushes
Paint rollers
Scrub brushes
Sponges

Rotating Materials
Eggbeaters
Water wheels
Wire whisks

Connecting and Disconnecting Materials
Clear tubing
Connectors
Funnels
Pipe tubes

Natural Materials (good for sink and float)
Corks
Driftwood
Rocks
Seashells
Twigs

Pretend Play Materials
Boats
Dishes
Dolls and baby clothes
Miniature rubber animals (frogs, fish, whales)

Water Wall Bases
Fence
Lattice
Plywood
Side of a building or shed
Wood pallet

Water Wall Materials
Buckets
Clear tubing
Fittings
Funnels
Hoses
Pipes
Plastic jugs or bottles
Rain gutters
Tubes

Cozy Spaces Tools and Materials

Creating Softness and Privacy
Bedsheets
Blankets
Body pillows
Canopies
Canopy netting
Comforters
Crib mattress
Cushions
Drop cloths
Fabrics
Large umbrellas
Parachutes
Pillows
Porch swing on the ground
Quilts
Rugs
Sheer outdoor curtains
Shower curtains

Loose Parts
Acorns
Bottle caps
Buttons
CDs
Cedar rings
Cinnamon sticks
Corks
Driftwood (small pieces)
Eucalyptus pods
Film canisters
Glass stones
Jar lids
Keys
Leaves
Liquid amber tree or sweet-gum tree balls
Marker caps
Metal washers
Pieces of old jewelry
Pine cones
Pom-poms
Sea glass
Seashells
Seed pods
Sticks
Stones
Tiles
Tree blocks
Tree cookies
Wooden maple rings
Wooden thread spools

Connecting and Disconnecting
Bark
Clothespins
Combs
Hangers
Jars and lids

Nuts and bolts
Ribbon
Rope
Scarf hangers
Shoelaces
Sock hangers
String
Velcro rollers
Wire
Yarn
Zip ties

Inserting
Bowls
Boxes
Bracelets
Candle holder with holes
Coffee pod holder
Colanders
Containers
Cups
Dowels
Felted rings
Hair donuts
Hair scrunchies
Keys and locks
Letter holder
Maple wood rings
Metal canning rings
Napkin rings
Paper towel holder
Pipe cleaners
Plate holder
Puzzles
Scarf holder
Tin cans
Tissue box
Tubes

References

Almon, Joan. 2013. *Adventure: The Value of Risk in Children's Play*. Annapolis, MD: Alliance for Childhood.

Brussoni, Mariana, Lise Olsen, Ian Pike, and David Sleet. 2012. "Risky Play and Children's Safety: Balancing Priorities for Optimal Child Development." *International Journal of Environmental Research and Public Health* 9: 3134–48.

Casey, Theresa, and Juliet Robertson. 2019. *Loose Parts Play*. 2nd ed. Edinburgh: Inspiring Scotland.

Chawla, Louise. 2015. "Benefits of Nature Contact for Children." *Journal of Planning Literature* 30, no. 4 (July): 433–52.

Coster, Denise, and Josie Gleeve. 2008. *Give Us a Go! Children and Young People's Views on Play and Risk-Taking*. www.playday.org.uk/wp-content /uploads/2015/11/give_us_a_go____children_and_young_peoples_views _on_play_and_risk_taking.pdf.

Halliday, M. A. K. 2004. *The Language of Early Childhood*. Edited by Jonathan J. Webster. New York: Continuum.

Iltus, Selim, and Roger Hart. 1995. "Participatory Planning and Design of Recreational Spaces with Children." *Architecture & Behaviour* 10, no. 4: 361–70.

Jambor, Tom. 1995. "Coordinating the Elusive Playground Triad: Managing Children's Risk-Taking Behavior, (While) Facilitating Optimal Challenge Opportunities, (within) a Safe Environment." Presented at the International Conference on Playground Safety, University Park, PA, October 10, 1995. https://files.eric.ed.gov/fulltext/ED405132.pdf.

Law, Suzanna, and Morgan Leichter-Saxby. 2015. *Loose Parts Manual: The DIY Guide to Creating a Playground in a Box*. Australia: Playground Ideas. www.popupadventureplay.org/wp-content/uploads/2019/08/Loose -Parts-Manual.pdf.

Leichter-Saxby, Morgan, and Jill Wood. 2018. "Comparing Injury Rates on a Fixed Equipment Playground and an Adventure Playground." United Kingdom: Pop-Up Adventure Play. https://popupadventureplaygrounds.files .wordpress.com/2018/02/parish-just-the-facts-final.pdf.

Sandseter, Ellen Beate Hansen. 2007. "Categorizing Risky Play—How Can We Identify Risk-Taking in Children's Play?" *European Early Childhood Education Research Journal* 15, no. 2 (January): 237–52. https://doi .org/10.1080/13502930701321733.

———. 2011. "Children's Risky Play in Early Childhood Education and Care." *ChildLinks* 3:2–6. www.researchgate.net/publication/275039981.

Sandseter, Ellen Beate Hansen, Rasmus Kleppe, and Ole Johan Sando. 2021. "The Prevalence of Risky Play in Young Children's Indoor and Outdoor Free Play." *Early Childhood Education Journal.* https://doi.org/10.1007 /s10643-020-01074-0.

Sawyers, Janet K. 1994. "The Preschool Playground: Developing Skills through Outdoor Play." *Journal of Physical Education, Recreation & Dance* 65, no. 6 (August): 31–33.

United States Consumer Product Safety Commission. 2015. *Public Playground Safety Handbook.* Bethesda, MD: USCPSC.

United States Environmental Protection Agency. 2019. "Public Webinar: Part 1— Tire Crumb Rubber Characterization." www.epa.gov/chemical-research /public-webinar-part-1-tire-crumb-rubber-characterization.

Wijk, Nikolien van. 2008. *Getting Started with Schemas: Revealing the Wonder- full World of Children's Play.* Christchurch, New Zealand: The New Zealand Playcentre Federation.

Willoughby, Marie. 2011. "The Value of Providing for Risky Play in Early Childhood Settings." *ChildLinks* 3:7–10. www.researchgate.net /publication/275039981_CHILDREN'S_RISKY_PLAY_IN_EARLY _CHILDHOOD_EDUCATION_AND_CARE.